T0019902

Make A Marriage,
Relationship and Family Last

"Gerard Muttukumaru gives readers the wisdom to decide to save their marriage or choose divorce as a last resort. Gerard's multi-cultural experiences are remarkably insightful and that makes this book a must-read."

-- Lee Raffel, M.S.W., L.M.F.T

Author of *Should I Stay or Go? How Controlled Separation Can Save You.* Lee has contributed to *The Today Show, Good Morning New York, O (Oprah Magazine), The Wall Street Journal, Ladies Home Journal, The Chicago Tribune* and *The Los Angeles Times.*

"This book will help bring harmony within one's home benefiting both parents and children. I recommend this book to all persons starting a family and even the veterans who have weathered some storms."

-- M. Ganesan MD, Professor and Psychiatrist

"... an excellent multicultural initiative from the author with concepts on how to strengthen your relationship with your partner."

-- Dr. Rocio Arias Soto MA, PhD, Psychologist, (Costa Rica)

"A wonderful and thought-provoking book for any couple that wants to improve their relationship."

-- Dr. Usha Gunawardana, MD, DPM (UK)

Make A Marriage,
Relationship and Family Last

A guide for intended
or married couples in any culture

Gerard D. Muttukumaru

An excellent and thought provoking book for any couple
that wants to improve their relationship

Polimedia
Publishing

All Polimedia titles, imprints, and distributed lines are available at special quantity discounts for bulk purchases for sales promotion, premiums, fund-raising, educational, or institutional use.

Special book excerpts or customized printings can also be created to fit specific needs. For details, write or contact the office of Polimedia Publishing:

Polimedia Publishing
440 S. El Cielo Road ste.#3-670
Palm Springs, CA 92262
info@polimediaent.com
www.polimediaent.com

2 3 4 5 6 7 8 9 10

Published by Polimedia Publishers
© 2010 Gerard D. Muttukumaru

ISBN-13: 978-0-9768617-8-2

Printed in the United States

To Melissa and Alexandra…
that they make wise choices.

And to every intended and married couple
who read this book. I hope and pray that
their lives are touched for the better.

"You raise me up; to more than I can be"

– Lyrics by Brendan Graham

I am grateful to everyone in so many countries who have touched me in my life and made this book possible. To the many psychiatrists, psychologists, mental health professionals, marriage counselors, and to the ordinary and extraordinary couples who in their own way also contributed to the book, a heartfelt thank you. My friend and colleague, Mrs. Shanthi Wijesinghe, a parenting and child development specialist in South Asia contributed a very meaningful chapter. She has my gratitude.

Table of Contents

Preface

This book was born out of adversity. It is deeply personal. It addresses what I consider to be arguably the most critical social problem, or even crisis, facing the West and global village. Marriage and family are the bedrock or foundation of any society.

The increasing breakdown of the institution of marriage and family is not anything to laugh at or be cynical about. People's lives are at stake. The future of innocent children is at stake. Marriage is a sacred institution. It must be preserved.

The choice of a life partner is perhaps the single most important decision any human being makes. In many cultures, the parents and family make this choice for their adult child. Sometimes this works well, sometimes it does not. The US and societies in the West are now increasingly multicultural. The US has always been a "nation of immigrants". Our universities and organizations are now filled with young people from nearly every corner of the planet. They meet, fall in love and get married or simply live together as partners. We must remember that cultures are neither right nor wrong. They just are. We must accept them. This book addresses the inter-cultural challenges in marriage and families and the critical issues that couples must address before they embark on their journey together. Questions for discussion and reflection for intended and married partners are provided as a conclusion to many chapters.

After the journey together has begun, several challenges confront each partner as individuals and as couples. This book is not a cure-all or a miracle; rather it is a simple guide that will hopefully make life together meaningful and joyful.

Marriage demands very hard and often painful work. In many societies, confronting and resolving issues that separate individuals with love is not taught and is often avoided. When these issues explode, serious problems arise and partners live in misery or in separate worlds. Many choose avoidance and suffer in silence. We have one life to live on this planet and we must live it fully and joyfully. It is my hope that this book brings some joy to couples before and after they have embarked on their journey together.

Heraclitus, the Greek philosopher, told us, "The only constant in life is change."

Change can only begin with each one of us. So many couples spend their lives trying to change the other person. This must end. We have control only of ourselves. Couples must have a total focus on helping each other become more than each can be. We must build each other up, every day, as a couple.

‖ The Global Marriage & Family Crisis

The seed for this book was planted a week before Christmas in 1996, by my then five year old daughter, who asked me after I kissed her goodbye outside our home in a suburb of Los Angeles, "Daddy, why don't you ever spend Christmas with us?" How does a father answer such a question from a beautiful five-year-old child, when there is so much emotion involved? My older daughter and I decided that given the situation between my ex-wife and I, especially during the Christmas season, that it was best for me to leave and spend the season with my brother, sister and cousins on the East Coast.

This book is born out of adversity and pain, which happen to be the greatest teachers in life. A friend in Asia, with advanced degrees in Christianity, Buddhism and psychology, graciously consented to read the first manuscript. After reading it, he took the time to sit down with me and share his thoughts.

He said to me, "Gerard, this book is too American. In addition, a reader in this part of the world might wonder what gives you the right to address this topic when you have failed in your first marriage? Failure is not accepted here." I really thought about this.

As a South Asian born American, it dawned on me how much influence America, (not England, Europe or Australia) has in every part of the world with its number one export, American culture in the form of Hollywood (even Bollywood, India was named after it!) . This cultural invasion can be seen in fashion, television programs such as 24, *Dynasty, Dallas, Sex and the City, Friends, Bold and the Beautiful, Baywatch,* CNN, the internet, *Google, Yahoo, Microsoft* and yes, two iconic brands, *Coca Cola* and *Victoria's Secret.*

In my professional life, I am a student, teacher, consultant and practitioner of global business, marketing, cross-cultural management, leadership, change, organizational culture and of how people behave in organizations. In this context it is interesting to note that over 75% of the world's most admired brands are American and yes they are fully integrated into our lives.

Just imagine the impact of these brands on every consumer in the world, especially the huge mass of consumers at "the bottom of the pyramid." This cultural invasion of America, which many resist or say they resist, impacts virtually every aspect of our lives no matter where we live. Angelina Jolie, Brad Pitt and George Clooney are now frequent visitors to refugee camps in Africa. Don't the terribly sad men, women and children in these camps want to look like them and imitate them? Even the poorest girl in the world, wants to yes, eat first, but also look like a Hollywood star and wear what they wear, even *Victoria's Secret*! *Microsoft* and *Google* dominate internet cafes in the most remote corners of the world!

So I really do not agree with my friend who felt the book was "too American". But he made me think. For better or worse, the "American Invasion" is seen and felt everywhere.

This cultural invasion has also severely eroded long held and even sacred family and religious values around the world. And strikes at the very heart of the institution of marriage and family in these countries. Several internal factors within the countries themselves have also contributed to this erosion. Married couples now see options available to them and choose to either stay or leave a marriage. American TV dramas tell them that divorce is not so bad after all. More and more couples think to themselves, "the bold, the beautiful and the powerful all do it!" so why can't I.

Experts in less developed countries tell me that marital problems and divorce have increased at an alarming rate. *Time Magazine Asia* ran a cover story in April 2004 titled, "Marriage Meltdown – Why Asia's Divorce Rates are Hitting All-Time Highs." In 2002, the divorce rate in South Korea, according to *Time Research*, was 47%; Hong Kong 41%; Japan 38%; Singapore 26%; and China 15%. I wonder what it will be in 2011!

Even in conservative Buddhist Thailand, divorces are on the increase because the younger generation has been brought up differently. This generation is more individualistic. When they get married, if there is a problem, they think more of their own interests instead of family harmony. In the overwhelmingly Catholic Philippines, where divorce is not allowed, the grounds for the annulment of a marriage have been widened to include cases where one partner has a low IQ, and legislation was enacted to speed up the annulment process! For non-Catholics reading this, annulment is what really ends a marriage in the eyes of the Catholic Church. It says that a marriage never existed in the first place! Interesting. What is more intriguing is that women not men, are increasingly taking the initiative in Asian countries to split up!

My friend who commented on my manuscript should think about the following observation by a Taiwanese marriage counselor who said, "Couples in Asia are more like American couples nowadays."

Have I failed in marriage? Perhaps. Failure like beauty is in the eyes of the beholder, but the price I paid compels me to try and stop every destructive argument and verbal abuse between a husband and wife, parent and child, from Los Angeles, California to Kuala Lumpur, Malaysia and beyond.

What is more, when I see this type of behavior between parents in the presence of their child/children, a sword pierces my heart. It's because I have been there. I guess this gives me some right to share my thoughts and feelings in this book with the hope that one person; a husband, a wife, or a child's life is made better. It is said, "Only people who have been through fire, see the price of destruction. Often, only they, not the complacent, act."

I also believe very strongly that a society which does not tolerate, embrace and learn from failure, will never really grow and prosper. The buzz word in the world of global business today is innovation or creativity. No real innovation or creativity can occur if individuals are terrified to fail. Trial and error, and yes, failure must be encouraged. It is OK to fail if one learns from it and reaches greater heights. The education systems in less developed nations do not encourage or tolerate failure. This also contributes to countries like Sri Lanka having one of the highest suicide rates in the world. Sri Lanka is not alone in this. Even in Japan, the second most powerful economy in the world, failure often leads to suicide even at the highest levels.

The greatest discoveries and movements in the world were the result of failure, driven by frail, humble human beings. The critic takes us nowhere. The person who makes the world a better place is the one in the arena who tries, fails and tries again; who remains humble, tolerant and accepting of other's failures and frailties. In the context of marriage, failure can be the best teacher.

As a result of my experience, I recommend divorce to no one. It is perhaps the greatest untold tragedy in the world. You, as the reader, do not have to accept anything I say. Some thoughts may be considered as provocative, irreverent, absurd or as pure fantasy. What I would like, is for the reader to gain something good and positive out of this book, which will make their marriage better or each partner a better human being. I know I have tried to make a complex subject simple, maybe even too simple.

This book is also for those husbands and wives, who together put on a terrific show for the world, but are different people in their own homes, and yes, even in their own bedrooms. How do they face their inner selves? Do they care?

Are husbands and wives running from each other? Do they prefer spending time with friends or at work, rather than with each other? For whom are we putting on the show? In this short life, is it worth all the effort? How can we claim to have a conversation with a higher being if we cannot have a conversation with our husbands, wives, parents and children? Do you think the "higher being" listens to our prayers if we are unable to talk to our spouses?

I have just stated that I recommend divorce to no one. However, there are four exceptions where divorce may be the only option:

1. It must take two to tango. Both partners must want to stay married, be it for themselves, for the children, for money, for family or for business reasons. I can hear my sanity being questioned, but in the global village in which we find ourselves, there are as

many reasons to get married and stay married, as there are people.

2. One chooses to be in a given situation, for whatever reasons, we must not be judgmental of other human beings. Each person has his or her own reasons for doing what he or she does. As Danny De Vito, so eloquently, put it in the film Renaissance Man, "The choices we make, dictate the life we live."

3. When there is physical violence or physical abuse, or the threat of it, by either partner, the two individuals should not be under the same roof. This is particularly so when young children witness abuse between parents. When either partner is excessively verbally abusive of the other, the two individuals should not live under the same roof.

4. When children are involved and if abuse of any kind is directed at the children, and this is found to be irreparable, then divorce may be the option.

I realize I have given four possible reasons for divorce but the relationship may still be "fixable." All other situations are resolvable, once destructive passions are eliminated. Too many life-changing decisions are made in the heat of passion. I also believe that if we, as a society and a people, take certain steps, idealistic as this may sound, the four reasons may also be eliminated. Deep and incurable psychiatric, psychological and pathological conditions may be an exception. Even when these exist, couples choose to remain in the marriage for economic, family, social, religious and other reasons "until death do they part". They then live separate lives under the same roof.

‖ The Celebration of Life & Marriage

The two parent family is the fundamental unit of any civiliza-tion. Nations and societies, indeed entire civilizations, are almost always destroyed, not from without, but from within. In the "new world order," at the time of the inception of this book, there ap-peared to be one enemy with a face, Saddam Hussein. He was eliminated. Now the face of evil has been given one name, Osama Bin Laden. The others are referred to in general terms such as, *rogue states, sponsors of terrorism* (though we now have our own to fear) etc. Castro in Cuba, Kim in North Korea, Assad in Syria, Ahmadinejad in Iran, they are no longer enemies out to destroy both America and the free world. Rhetoric and threats do not always lead to destructive action. A global survey conducted in 2007, identified President George Bush as the greatest perceived threat to humanity. This is the view from outside of America! None of these people are going to destroy our way of life. They cannot. The sad thing is, we appear to be destroying ourselves.

As a great general once discovered, "We have seen the enemy, and it is us."

Yes, there are those who believe that we are getting better and better as a people. Politicians reinforce this when it is time to cam-paign, but the reality is that we, as a global society, have never been faced with greater challenges, especially in the context of marriage, family, our children, abuse in all its forms, illegal drug use, racism, crime, violence, hatred for our brothers, and yes, globalization and the global village. In light of all the issues, it is the preservation of marriage and family that must be central in order for us to continue getting better as human beings and as a society.

Something is wrong in a great nation such as the US, when a spouse, lover or friend physically abuses a woman every nine se-conds. Something is wrong when less than 5% of the world's population (the US), consumes almost 70% of the world's narcotics. Something is wrong when *Time Magazine* ran a cover story entitled "The most violent nation on earth – the US." The violence this story referred to, included all forms of violence, even the reported instances of child and domestic abuse. There are more violent societies especially among poorer nations and failed societies where so much violence from personal disputes, suicide, spousal and child abuse go unreported. The city of Johannesburg is a sad story. Nations ravaged by war are in a totally different category.

Someone once said, "There are lies, damn lies and statistics." So, I don't know how true all of this is. I think most people know, deep down, that we are all faced with some serious challenges.

No challenge is greater than the challenge of preserving the family. Most of our problems as a society can be traced in one way or another to the breakup of the family. For the sake of preserving the family, a family should not continue as it is if there is no respect between parents and verbal abuse is witnessed by children. The issues must be addressed and resolved. The scars suffered by children who live under these conditions are often irreparable. Children learn what they live and live what they learn.

A survey by the *Knight Ridder* news organization, revealed that Americans spend more time watching TV and getting their information from this source, than all other activities combined. Today, the internet competes with TV for this attention. In some of the most remote areas of the world, where there is no access to a computer or the internet, you often find a TV set where teledramas or soap operas are the only source of entertainment. Consider their impact on children and the family unit. The "novellas" in Latin America and teledramas and soap operas around the rest of the world, have spouses and adults yelling at each other, sometimes hitting and throwing things at each other, and even walking away from marriages for the stupidest of reasons! Anyone watching them can see that they don't have any trouble sleeping around with each other's partners and the youth of the world takes a page out of that book!

What masquerades as "news," are often the bad and the ugly. We rarely hear about those quiet saints in our communities and the larger global village, which go about doing good in their own way.

The New York Times of January 5, 1998, ran a story titled, "In Place of the Abused – a doctor works in the grim world of battered children." The story was about a remarkable woman and human being, Dr. Linda Cahill, Medical Director of the *Child Protection Center at Montefiore Medical Center* in the Bronx, New York.

The article stated, "The number of such [child abuse] cases is on the rise in the city and around the nation, with more children than ever enduring abuse and neglect."

"Experts believe that 85% of abuse-related deaths are not reported, are misidentified as accidental or disease related or are attributed to other "erroneous causes." These are not "cases" to us. These are children...I truly believe that the dissolution of the family, the failure of the family in our society, is the essential feature in this... the roots are pretty obvious," Dr. Cahill says. What an extraordinary woman!

I have met and witnessed the work of so many souls like Dr. Cahill when I served on the Board of Catholic Charities in two Southern California cities, in my role as Asia Program Manager, based in Manila, Philippines, for one of the largest NGO's (Non-Governmental Organization) in the world, *World Vision International* and in my travels all over the world. The work of extraordinary individuals, volunteers, social workers, nuns, priests, and missionaries, in the most remote corners of the world, and even in aboriginal villages where I stayed, all profoundly influenced me.

It is abundantly clear that the number one priority of any nation, as a civilized society, should be the preservation and celebration of life, marriage and the family. In the most powerful nation on earth, the US, I call upon the President and the leadership of the Senate and House, to convene a special session of Congress, or even a high profile, "crisis conference" in the White House, to give this challenge center stage. Leaders in other nations should also set the example. A primary function of any leader is to champion life, marriage and family. Would an elected official dare oppose this? The citizens must demand this priority. The government can lead and bring the issue to a nation's consciousness. It cannot solve the problem. Individual fathers, mothers, families, teachers, clergy, business and community leaders must. Let's all end the blame game. "We have met the enemy and it is us." We must change from within.

This is also a book about faith and hope. We can change as a society and as a people if we truly believe in the words of the song *Let there be peace on earth and let it begin with me.* If we start with ourselves, one person at a time, and one community at a time, the politicians will follow. What we need is a revolution of the family, of the heart, of the soul, that propels us to echo, with gentleness and humility, the words of the great American Senator Robert Dole, "Where is the outrage?" Let us begin as we read this book. Let us turn to everyone, every soul we have hurt or abused and say, "I am sorry. I love you. I need your help."

And, yes, it takes a village and more to make a marriage work. We all have a stake in each marriage, especially among our own families. Adults often behave like children. Every adult has a child within and it surfaces often because growing up is so hard to do.

The greatest sin condemned by a spiritual Master was not adultery, but rather, pride, indifference and self-righteousness. To maintain the attitude of, "I don't care" or "I don't want to get involved," or, to refer the immortal words of Clark Gable in the classic film *Gone With the Wind*, "Frankly my dear, I don't give a damn!" We are accountable for what we do and what we fail to do. I believe that all faiths demand that we care and that we do give a damn. When a marriage is in trouble within our own families, we see adults acting as children. As individuals and members of the family we must care and we must act.

On a global scale, it took the Catholic Church, decades to finally ask for forgiveness from the Jewish people for staying silent during the holocaust. The Catholic Church had failed to speak out against this unbelievable crime against humanity. Silence in the face of terrible wrong and injustice is a great sin. The late Pontiff John Paul II, a towering figure in recent history, had the courage to confess this sin to the Jewish people and the world. Shouldn't we, when we witness this in our own families, organizations, in society and in our countries, without passing judgment, speak out and correct the wrong and injustice? We must also learn to separate the "sin from the sinner." We must love the sinner and reject the sin. After all, we are human and eventually we all fail. The immortal words uttered on the sands of the Middle East by one of the greatest spiritual Masters over 2000 years ago come to mind, "He that is without sin, let him cast the first stone."

This book is by no means a definitive work. It is written out of pain and struggle by a soul that has been wounded by the trauma of divorce. I wish the same on no one. A reader may think I'm crazy for some of my ideas. I am not a mental health professional but part of my academic specialization was in the field of organizational behavior. In addition, I have counseled and have been involved, by choice and otherwise, in the lives of so many young people, older people, executives and managers, and couples both in the workplace and in families.

We must seek the best help. I believe it was the father of American psychiatry, Dr. Karl Menninger who said, "If all persons lived by the Ten Commandments, our profession may cease to exist!" All I ask is that you share this journey with me as a fellow pilgrim in this fragile, short-lived journey we call life and marriage.

Too many of the books on marriage, divorce and relationships, are too complicated for the average person to digest, especially with the time constraints of raising a family, making a living and meeting the challenges of day to day life. I will strive to keep this book as simple and as digestible as possible. None of us have actually arrived (though several of us, especially teenagers and twenty-something's, think they have!). Which married person does not want to make his or her marriage better? We are all learning and hopefully, want to become better marriage partners and human beings.

As we begin, here are some questions for partners to ponder in order to make a marriage or any relationship, all that it can be and more.

PERSONAL REFLECTION AND DISCUSSION
BETWEEN PARTNERS

Q: What does marriage mean to me?

A: _____

Q: What kind of relationship did I see and experience between my parents? How did it affect me?

A: _____

_____

Q: Do I see the "bad" things in my father or mother in me? If yes, what are they?

A: _____

_____

Q: Do I see this in the way I treat and communicate with my spouse?

A: _____

_____

Q: What am I willing to do to change this within myself?

A: _____

_____

Q: In choosing my partner, what are the five reasons I had for marrying him or her?

A: _____

_____

Q: Would I marry my partner again for the same reasons? Any new reasons?

A: _____

_____

Q: Am I willing to change anything within myself to have a healthier, happier and better marriage? Do I owe this to myself?

A: _____

_____

Q: What five things am I willing to change within me?

A: _____

_____

RULE ONE:
It Takes Two to Tango

During the Persian Gulf Crisis, just prior to *Operation Desert Storm*, the world was on edge. Was the US led coalition going to declare war on Iraq or not? As a last minute attempt at a diplomatic solution to the crisis, the world's top diplomat, then UN Secretary General Javier Perez de Cuellar, flew to Baghdad to meet with the Iraqi leadership. After a closed-door session, the Secretary General, came out and faced the world press. If I remember right, he said, "I love to dance. But it takes two to tango." There wasn't a diplomatic solution and war seemed inevitable.

Marriage is not very different. At its best, it is a beautiful life-long dance. It must take both partners to want to make it work. It takes two to tango. The tango, which originated in Latin America, is arguably one of the most difficult dances to learn. It demands harmony between both partners.

Unless a partner is in a marriage for reasons other than love, perhaps money, business, or children, it takes both to want to make it work. I had the honor of taking a walk with a renowned Jesuit priest who led numerous retreats around the US for couples and for corporations.

He shared with me that whenever he received a request for marriage counseling, he placed one condition before even the first session. The condition was that he would only meet the couple if both partners wanted to make the marriage work and that both partners were willing to do everything that it took to make it work.

This, my Jesuit friend disclosed, eliminated at least half of the couples that wanted to meet with him. Why? Because the other half was typical of individuals who either wanted to rationalize the split, dump on the other partner, or merely wanted to go through the ritual to satisfy the other partner and/or the family.

We must first want to be healed, to tango together, if we are to make a marriage work.

Bill, a man I met during a management retreat that I was leading, held a management position in a large multinational organization and was based in Los Angeles. He was one of forty-five managers who participated in the retreat at a resort in Southern California. The focus of the retreat was on building a world class leadership team and also to address some serious cross-cultural issues between managers. Since the retreat was spread over three days, several of the participants brought their wives, some even their children. I observed that Bill was "not there," for he was only physically present at the sessions. It was obvious he was troubled. For some reason he connected with me, and when the time was right he approached me with his concerns.

"Can we chat alone?" he asked me during a break. I agreed. What surfaced was that he had an affair with his secretary when away on business and his wife had not forgiven him.

He loved his wife, but she was insistent on a separation. Bill had brought both his wife and his daughter to the retreat. I asked if I could meet with his wife alone in the lobby. She confessed that she could not trust him again and was openly hostile towards him. Bill wanted to work things out with her, but she was very reluctant. He wanted to tango but she did not.

They were both lovely and very gifted people. Their eighteen year old daughter was gorgeous. Bill's wife spoke eight languages! She now had to be willing to learn a "new language," in essence, the tango.

I spent an hour on the third day of the retreat with both of them and I sensed that some of her hostility had been diffused. One question I asked both of them together was, "What attracted both of you to each other in the first place?" I felt that the answers each gave in the presence of the other, in some way reconnected them.

Bill's situation with his wife needed some serious work. Both accepted that the journey ahead, of rebuilding trust in each other,

16

was a hard and painful one. But they now appeared willing to tango. I referred them to a good friend who was a superb psychotherapist in the Los Angeles area. Today, they are still together. Bill showed up at an executive education class I taught on Global Business Strategy four years later and shared with me that he and his wife are more in love with each other than ever. What did I do? I was merely there at the right moment, in the same way some have been there for me in my journey.

I hope readers learn something from Bill and his wife. It takes two to tango. Two souls who are willing and committed to resolve problems together and to dance together in the harmony in their marriage. The tango, as I stated earlier, is a tough dance to learn.

PERSONAL REFLECTION AND DISCUSSION
BETWEEN PARTNERS

Q: Do I know myself? Have I met myself? Do I know what this means? Who am I really?

A: _____

_____

Q: Am I happy with myself? If yes, why? If no, why not?

A: _____

_____

Q: Do I have joy within me? Do I know the difference between happiness and joy?

A: _____

Q: Do I spend time alone with myself in reflection or prayer?

A: _____

_____

Q: What do I want to do with my life and the talents and gifts given to me?

A: _____

_____

Q: What are my dreams? Have I shared them with my partner?

A: _____

_____

Q: What are my strengths? Weaknesses? Have I shared them with my partner?

A: _____

_____

Q: What are my partner's strengths and weaknesses? Are we both willing and able to build each other up every day and help each other overcome any weaknesses with respect, without putting the other down?

A: _____

_____

Q: Do we believe and accept that there is no such thing as a "perfect" partner?

A: _____

_____

Q: What five things am I willing to change within, beginning today, to tango with my partner in marriage?

A: _____

_____

RULE TWO:
Zero Expectations

I have had the privilege of serving on the visiting faculty of several MBA and International Executive/Professional Education Programs in several universities in California, as well as addressing management forums worldwide. An obsession for the past several years and even now is Quality Management or to use a technical term, "Six Sigma." The objective of this exercise is to strive to manufacture a product with zero or near zero defects. This is a necessary objective in production and business and is critical to business success in the hyper competitive global economy of today.

I believe that life becomes a lot easier, when we enter into a romantic or marriage relationship, expecting nothing from our partner, that is, with zero expectations. Do I sound crazy? I hope not. My friends in the business of psychotherapy and counseling, the "gurus," and the marriage or relationship experts tell us that we must enter into marriage relationship with "realistic" expectations. Realistic for whom, I ask? One partner's realism may not be the others. So the debate on what is realistic and what is not, may rage on right through the marriage. This is often accompanied by a regular weekly visit to the therapist.

In the global village in which we live, with an increasing number of cross-cultural or intercultural, and inter-religious marriages, what is "realistic" may differ from culture to culture, from religion to religion and from person to person. I have some understanding of this having studied, lived and worked in numerous countries around the world. The majority of my life has been spent in multicultural situations and in non-Christian societies. I have also taught cross-cultural management and communication. Make no mistake. I understand the critical role of meeting and exceeding expectations between the various stakeholders in organizations, employees, customers, shareholders, and society.

But marriage is a totally different matter. To the world, it is a contract. But in the eyes of the "one," who most people believe created the world and brings people together; marriage is a sacred union between two persons or souls. As the American country singer Hank Snow, put it: *Married by the Bible, divorced by the law*! When things are terribly wrong in a marriage, one should not run from church to church, mosque to mosque, temple to temple, guru to guru, hoping for a miracle. Marriage or any romantic relationship demands very hard and painful work between partners and within oneself. "The miracle" must first start inside each of us.

When we have zero expectations of the other, and focus all our energies on accepting and loving the other for what he or she is, the marriage relationship can become a beautiful tango or waltz. We are all frail human beings. Life does strange things to people. Life in the US and other advanced societies has become an incredible challenge to ordinary citizens. In the US, the not so ordinary Americans, especially the Hollywood elite and super rich, are also severely challenged in their marriages and relationships. Stress has become the number one killer in the US. This is in a society known for arguably the best quality of life and highest standard of living on this planet!

My Australian and Scandinavian friends may disagree. All of this takes a toll on each of us as we try to live together in a marriage and raise a family.

US News and *World Report*, within the December 29th, 1997 issue, had an interesting feature story about one aspect of the US as a society. It said, "Americans are the fattest people on earth and they're rapidly getting fatter. One in three adults is obese, as are a fifth of all children. America grows more obese despite spinning classes, bran muffins, liposuction and Oprah."

Weight loss, dieting and fitness programs have become a national obsession. "We gotta have it!" is their mantra. This new trend takes a toll on the family. In my view, things have only got worse since this article was first printed.

I don't know why we say and do the terrible things we do to ourselves each other. We have to confront the demons within us by seeking professional help. Mahatma Gandhi once observed, "The only real devils in the world are those running around in our hearts."

Sociologists and psychologists continue to study why we do the terrible things we do to each other, in order to more fully understand the problem. It is critical that we first learn to be patient and tolerant of each other. We must understand that each one of us is trying to do the best we can. Often all we need is a hand, a smile, a word of encouragement, someone to care. There are also so many souls waiting to be taught how to love and forgive. For whatever reason, whether learned in childhood or through experience, these souls don't know how to love and moreover, how to forgive. This was brought out so powerfully in the film, *Walk in the Clouds*, when the father, filled with anger and hate, breaks down and pleads with his daughter to teach him how to love. "I don't know how," he confesses to her. "Teach me," he asks. He had worked his butt off for his family, but never learned how to love and to show it. How many of us wounded souls have the courage to confess this?

As you will read later in the book, so many people from twenty-four to eighty-four years of age, have not learned how to love as a result of severe emotional trauma. They have buried their capacity to love unconditionally.

How many homes have we walked into and found people yelling at each other? It is sad when families know no other way to communicate. Few people take the time to talk to each other. Even fewer listen. We yell and scream at each other. Sometimes we have gotten so used to it, that we have become numb or don't even know it's happening. We continue to "exist". Will we continue to yell and scream at our partner or child, if we knew he or she had only one week to live? Death is the greatest teacher in life. How ironic.

One of the best classifications of human beings can be found in the words of the beautiful song. "The Circle of Life," written by Tim Rice and sung by Elton John.

"....Some of us fall by the wayside:

some of us soar to the stars:

some of us sail through our troubles:

some have to live with the scars"

Think about it! Almost every human being I have met falls into one of these categories. These are the same people who are immersed in marriage relationships. Each of us is trying to be the best he or she can be. If we are not, our loved ones must, with genuine affection and love, encourage us and build us up. There is too much tearing down, cynicism, sarcasm and verbal abuse in our homes. I think it was in the film *Jerry Maguire*, the beautiful Dorothy confesses, "I love him for the man he is, and the man he almost is." In a marriage, we must expect nothing from each other, but spend every moment helping the other achieve their dreams.

In our daily living, in our kitchen, if a dish is not washed - wash it; if the trash is not emptied - empty it; if the floor is not swept - sweep it. Our partner may have forgotten to do it, or there may be a perfectly logical reason why he or she has not done it.

Life in most countries and urban cities is tough today for most people. In spite of what the politicians say, married partners have to work two and three jobs just to make ends meet in advanced societies. Married partners come home tired, stressed out and often, angry.

It's amazing what people do for each other when there is true love, sensitivity, concern, caring, respect and when asked in a beautiful way, "Can you do this for me?" It can be amazing how romantic washing a dish, taking the trash out or sweeping the floor can be, when there is love, romance, respect and "magic" in the air.

This has become so rare in our homes. We issue edicts, demands and to-do lists. Where is the romance in this? If there are children, the children must be trained with love and respect. Adults don't often need training, unless one is married to a spoiled brat! But then, the partners knew this during their dating phase. Yet they chose each other as life mates.

In military strategy, it is more prudent to ignore or avoid, border skirmishes and minor battles and focus totally on winning the war. The war must focus on putting romance back in our marriages and preserving them. How much time and energy do married partners spend on border conflicts and minor battles? It is so sad. But as a wise man once said, "A war must be won before it is fought." Or; "To win without fighting is best."

People with obsessive-compulsive disorders of varying degrees cannot wait. They must have everything cleaned, arranged and done NOW. Any disruption in their schedule causes them to react very strongly, even irrationally.

Hilda is an eighty-four year old woman and cannot wait. She must have everything now. She is Catholic and falls apart if she is five minutes late for mass! "What will the priest think?" she asks in agitation.

When I mentioned this to the priest who knows her, he laughed! "Look at the guilt you and your church has put into her, Father," I told him with my hand on his shoulder. He was thoroughly amused.

Waiting is hard. A renowned speaker in Hollywood, California, once said, "You can tell me to do anything and I probably will. But don't tell me to wait!"

We have to learn to find the balance between seizing the moment and waiting for the right moment. This can be totally misunderstood and used by an individual to justify not taking a risk and doing nothing. We know so many people who have waited all their lives to do something they should have done a long time ago. As Elvis aptly put it in song: "I've spent a lifetime, waiting for the right time.....it's now or never...my love can't wait."

We must not be "going to do" people who die with nothing done. There is a great tragedy in a life that might have been. We must dare to do what must be done today to restore a damaged marriage or relationship. This must be a mutual decision between both partners.

Every morning, the moment married partners wake up, they must look into each other's eyes and remind themselves how much in love they are with each other. Try this!

Have zero expectations of each other, each day, and help the other achieve his or her dreams. When there are zero expectations, any little thing that is done by one partner for the other, is valued and appreciated and builds the romance and relationship.

PERSONAL REFLECTION AND DISCUSSION BETWEEN PARTNERS

Q: Did I enter into my marriage with expectations of my partner? What were these expectations?

A: _____

_____

Q: Has my partner satisfied my expectations? If yes, how? If not, how?

A: _____

_____

Q: Have my expectations of my partner made me happy?

A: _____

_____

Q: Have my expectations of my partner caused conflict or put a strain on our relationship? If yes, what am I doing to improve our relationship regarding expectations?

A: _____

_____

Q: Am I willing to have zero or no expectations of my partner?

A: _____

_____

Q: Am I willing to accept my partner as he or she is and help the other become all that they can be?

A: _____

_____

Q: What five things within me am I willing to change beginning today to help my partner become all that he or she can be?

A: _____

_____

RULE THREE:
Be Best of Friends

"Greater love than this no man has, that a man lay down his life for his friend."

Friend. There is no sweeter word in any language and no greater gift or privilege. A true friend is one who is there no matter what. Being there, no matter what the situation, be it good or bad, is perhaps the greatest gift one soul can give to another; one partner in a marriage can give to the other. A true friend is the one still standing by you when you have lost everything. A true friend is one who accepts you as you are and helps you become all or more than you can be.

A few years ago, I happened to catch Larry King interviewing Tom Hanks. When Mr. King asked the actor about his wife, Tom Hanks continued to describe his wife as his best friend. My soul is touched each time I see two partners in a marriage describe each other as best friends and lovers.

Best friends, as I have said, accept each other as they are. True love, respect, caring and compassion for each other characterize their relationship. They see and bring out the best in each other. Stories of true friendship have been immortalized in poetry, prose, song, dance, theatre and film. Best friends do not sit in judgment of each other. They listen and try to understand. They uplift and encourage. They do not put each other down. They help each other through the peaks and valleys of life, to grow and achieve each other's dreams. Marriage partners must be best friends if they are to blossom together and celebrate the dance of life.

In the film *The Wedding Planner*, the father tells his daughter, why he married her mother. "Appreciation turned to respect, respect turned to like, and like turned to love." You will read more of this in a subsequent chapter, "What Music Can Teach Us."

PERSONAL REFLECTION AND DISCUSSION
BETWEEN PARTNERS

Q: What does "best friend" mean to me?

A: _____

_____

Q: Is my partner my best friend? Why?

A: _____

_____

Q: Do my partner and I bring out the best in each other?

A: _____

_____

Q: Do I share my deepest thoughts and feelings with my partner? What thoughts and feelings do I not share with my partner? Why?

A: _____

_____

Q: Do we enjoy being with each other?

A: _____

_____

Q: What are my deepest fears? Have I shared them with my partner as my best friend?

A: _____

_____

Q: Do I prefer to be in the company of my friends or "in a crowd?"

A: _____

_____

Q: What am I willing to change within me to enjoy the company of my partner?

A: _____

_____

Q: Do I keep silent, fearing that I might say something nasty to my partner? Why is this? What am I afraid of? What am I doing to change myself to be able talk nicely to my partner? Do I think that by being silent I am improving our relationship?

A: _____

_____

Q: Do I see my partner as intellectually superior to me? Does this make me uncomfortable with my partner? If yes, what am I doing to learn from, encourage and support my partner in achieving our dreams together as one?

A: _____

_____

RULE FOUR:
Live in the Moment

The opening words of the film, *The Milagro Beanfield War*, directed by the legendary actor and director Robert Redford, were, "Thank you God, for giving me another day." Every day is a precious gift to us. Every moment.

I believe that every family in our global village can change, if each partner believes and accepts the reality that tomorrow, indeed the next moment, is guaranteed to no one. Today, the moment we live in, could be our last. This day, this moment, must be embraced and lived to the fullest, by each partner, and each child. We must forgive and be forgiven today. We must reconcile and be reconciled by those we may have hurt, offended or wronged, today. For this to occur, both parties must be willing participants. However, one has no control over the emotions or responses of another soul. Each partner must do what is right in his or her heart and soul.

It is said that the inability to admit failure and weakness, especially in a macho, feminist or success-obsessed society, is an obstacle to truly celebrating each moment. One of the hardest things to do is to forgive oneself and forgive another human being. The gurus tell us that forgiving oneself is the hardest. Several marital partners go through, or sail through life, crippled by this inability to forgive. It gets us nowhere. To truly celebrate each moment of a marriage we must continually forgive each other and strive to live in perfect harmony. Since we are all flawed human beings, living on this fragile planet and not in paradise, the operative word is "strive."

Loneliness terrifies us because we are afraid to face our innermost selves or souls. Some of us almost always want to be "in a crowd." It is safer. We are less vulnerable. But it is only in moments of solitude, that we can truly discover who we are as human beings.

Make A Marriage, Relationship and Family Last

It is when we are alone with our partner or a loved one, however terrifying as this may be to some, that we can truly discover the other.

It is said that the longest, most painful and most meaningful journey a human being can make, is deep into the recesses of his or her soul. Let each partner in a marriage celebrate such precious moments of solitude. It is only when we can celebrate moments of solitude, not in self-indulgence but in self-discovery that we can truly celebrate the time we have together with our best friend, lover, or marriage partner.

PERSONAL REFLECTION AND DISCUSSION BETWEEN PARTNERS

Q: Do I believe that every minute, every moment of my life, is a gift?

A: _____

_____

Q: Do I believe that my partner's life or my life could end any moment?

A: _____

_____

Q: Do we take time every day to do things together or spend time alone as a couple?

A: _____

34

Q: Do I yell at my partner every day? If yes, why? What am I willing to change within myself?

A: _____

_____

Q: Is there any suspicion between us? If yes, what am I suspicious of? Have you shared these suspicions with your partner?

A: _____

_____

Q: Do I know how to forgive my partner every day for what he or she may have said or done that caused me pain?

A: _____

_____

Q: Do I believe that every spiritual teacher has taught us that forgiveness and unconditional love are the foundation of any marriage or relationship?

A: _____

_____

Q: Do I go to bed angry with my partner? If yes, what am I going to do today to change this?

A: _____

_____

RULE FIVE:
Never Argue

You are likely to disagree with the next statement.

Best friends should not argue.

Best friends respect each other profoundly. When you respect another soul, you do not argue. You talk. You share. You listen. An argument usually occurs between two souls that really do not respect each other. I am told that arguing between lovers, between marriage partners is very sexy. That it can be excellent foreplay, which leads to passionate lovemaking. This is the subject for another book!

An argument by definition implies that one partner is not listening to the other. It can also be judgmental. Best friends are not judgmental of each other. They listen. They heed the words of grandmother Willow in the Disney classic *Pocahontas,* "Listen with your heart, and you will understand." Being there, without judging, is what best friends do.

We are all flawed human beings. We all fail at some point. Some fail more often than others. This may be because some just risk more than others. They are more adventurous than most. They are among those who have made great nations what they are today. In the world of business, they are called entrepreneurs or risk takers. Danger and risk are in their character, or even pathology. The greatest achievements and discoveries in life have been born out of failure. Those who risk nothing, never grow, and achieve little or nothing. Life is a risk.

When we fail as marriage partners, it is because we lose our sense of balance and harmony with our partner, our loved ones, ourselves and even the world. This failure often manifests itself in anger. When we are angry, we strike out at those closest or dearest to us. We argue. Often the first person in the line of fire is our marital partner. When this happens, it is very important that marriage partners should never let the sun go down on their anger. Never go to bed being angry at each other. Forgive, listen and be reconciled to each other and the world, before falling asleep. It's amazing how romantic and sexy this can be!

The book of James in the New Testament put it powerfully:

"Every kind of beast and bird, reptile and sea creature can be tamed, and has been tamed by humankind, but no human being can tame the tongue – a restless evil, full of deadly poison. With it we bless God and curse man who is made in his image. Out of the same mouth come praise and cursing".

How many of us would give anything to take back terrible words we have uttered to a loved one just seconds later?

On their way home after a pleasant dinner, Ken decided to share with his wife, a conversation he had with his friend Jonathan, a retired police officer.

"Jonathan seems to be so humble, but he always refers to junior officers in a condescending manner," he said to his wife.

Ken was not criticizing Jonathan, whom he liked and respected, but was simply sharing a very private observation with his wife. His wife, upon hearing this, snapped and a verbal tirade against Ken followed. It was an assault on Ken's character and life.

"I know you," she said. Ken was fifty and his wife forty-five. They had only known each other for 6 years! Did she really know her husband? Do we really know another person?

Wilfred and his brother Jerry had not stayed in touch since they were very young children. They were always in separate schools and for the last thirty-five years were separated by thirteen time zones.

Wilfred was the kind of man that thrived on converting most conversations into arguments, only to make a point. His talents were devoted to the judgment of others, both privately and publicly. He felt it was "his mission in life" to initiate investigations of what he believed was wrong doing. He demanded purity of others, while living a life of deception. He had engaged in criminal behavior but had not been caught.

When the brothers decided to reconnect during a visit, Wilfred turned his wrath on Jerry, and attempted to destroy him. Wilfred was a master at manipulating the truth to his advantage and accomplished this by deceptive and covert behavior that even his spouse was not aware of. Furthermore, his wrath was expressed publicly.

When did Wilfred's jealousy of his brother begin? Did it lay dormant during decades of separation?

Did he feel, even as a child, that Jerry was more favored by their parents? The parents, it was discovered, treated each of their four children equally. The destruction caused within the family and to Jerry by Wilfred was immeasurable.

Juanita called her husband Juan, who was home for the day, and asked him to purchase a ticket on her behalf to a concert that was being performed that evening. He did. She also called later that day and asked him to put some clothes in the washing machine. He did. However, Juan had forgotten that the dryer was not working properly and put the washed clothes into the dryer thinking everything was fine. Two hours later, when Juanita came home from the concert, she found the clothes in the broken dryer and yelled, "You are so stupid, you can do nothing right!" How deadly the tongue can be! The next morning Juanita went to her place of worship and sang praises to God with that same tongue!

Why do partners, friends and family members do this to each other? Each one of us must get to the root cause of such tirades, verbal assaults and wrath, and resolve them. I believe that the tongue can be tamed, at least to some extent. But how do we change the psychological DNA that drives an individual to destructive behavior?

I was a volunteer in some of the worst prisons in the US. What I have learned from these experiences, is that even in the worst of criminals, there is some good which must be drawn out.

There is no greater force to make this happen than the power of love, forgiveness, reconciliation, tolerance and acceptance of each other. This also brings about repentance. This was marvelously portrayed in the film *Dead Man Walking*.

The tongue turns negative thoughts into words and produces arguments. Arguments come from disillusioned hearts, not from love or unconditional acceptance. Accept individual differences and points of view. There are as many points of view as there are people on this planet. An American Indian saying reminds us to: "Never criticize a person till you have walked a mile in their shoes."

PERSONAL REFLECTION AND DISCUSSION
BETWEEN PARTNERS

Q: Do you feel arguments between partners are "normal?"

A: _____

_____

Q: Is it part of normal communication? Why?

A: _____

_____

Q: Do I argue with my partner often? Every day? If yes, does it help or hurt our relationship?

A: _____

_____

Q: What do I argue about with my partner?

A: _____

_____

Q: Do I argue to change my partner's thinking or behavior? If yes, must I always have my way?

A: _____

_____

Q: Can I imagine our marriage or relationship without arguments? What will it be like? Can I describe it?

A: _____

_____

Q: Do I respect my partner's opinions?

A: _____

_____

Q: Is my tongue full of deadly poison, a little bit of poison or is it filled with love and respect for my partner?

A: _____

_____

Q: Do I need to change anything about my tongue? If yes, what changes am I willing to make beginning today?

A: _____

_____

Q: Do I have a temper? If yes, where does this come from? Do I lose it often? Why?

A: _____

_____

Q: What changes will I make within me beginning today to control my temper?

A: _____

_____

RULE SIX:
Always Respect One Another

Respect for each other should be the cornerstone of any marriage. Where there is respect, most other ingredients fall into place. Every reader will know this, much more than I can ever attempt to explain. Each partner will know this to be true deep inside them, as they read this book.

Where there is respect between marriage partners, there is true love, caring, friendship, and the lovers are free to celebrate and enjoy every moment together.

In a TV profile of the incredibly gifted entertainer and human being, Gloria Estefan, her mother explains the marital relationship between her daughter, Gloria and her equally gifted husband, Emilio. "They are the best of friends and have a deep respect for each other...they do not do anything, without consulting with each other and listening to each other." Need I say more on the importance of respect?

When respect begins to cease between partners, they must recognize this, see the warning signs, try and restore it themselves or seek professional help.

PERSONAL REFLECTION AND DISCUSSION
BETWEEN PARTNERS

Q: Do I respect myself? If not, why? What am I willing to change within myself to respect myself first?

A: _____

Q: Do I respect my partner as a person? If no, when did this lack of respect begin? Did I respect him or her when I got married? If no, what five things in my partner do I not respect and why?

A: _____

_____

Q: Do I believe that that a marriage or any relationship can exist but not prosper and become all that it can be if there is no respect between partners?

A: _____

_____

Q: What five things within me am I willing to change, beginning today, to respect my partner?

A: _____

_____

Q: If my partner and I have children, do I know how badly they are affected if they do not see and experience respect between their parents?

A: _____

RULE SEVEN:
Listen, Listen, Listen

This step, in one way or another, flows through the entire book. Respect and listening, true genuine listening, is the glue that hold marriages together and help them grow, blossom and become all that they can be. Respect and listening can only occur, in a marriage relationship when there exists a profound love for each other.

Paul Tournier, a Swiss psychiatrist wrote, "Listen to most of the conversations in the world today. They are conversations of the deaf." Simon and Garfunkel in *The Sound of Silence* characterize our society when they sing, "People talking without speaking. People hearing without listening." How prophetic!

If the family is the fundamental unit of any civilization, then listening must take center stage among married partners, and yes, between parents and children, in every home in our global village. To put it bluntly, we need to shut up and listen to each other.

I believe, one of the reasons why the US supports the largest therapy or mental health industry in the world, is because we have stopped listening to each other. We pay good money to mental health professionals, only to learn how to listen. We are a great country – but are also the most disconnected, lonely and alienated, depressed and medicated society on earth!

A recent Wall Street Journal article went so far as to describe the US as "a nation of nuts!"

Our society is complex by nature. We have developed a culture in which fathers and mothers have disappeared and abandoned their primary responsibilities as parents. Almost anyone can become a father or mother, but so few know how to be parents.

Parenthood is the greatest responsibility in this world. I applaud President Bill Clinton and, presently, Secretary of State Hillary Clinton, for using the bully pulpit to stress this symbolically as well as by example with how they have raised their daughter Chelsea, who is now a fine young woman. We all watched as President Clinton put his family and the nation through the trials of his frailty. What is amazing is that the Clintons appear to have survived and overcome this as a family. What is baffling to me is the incredible popularity that President Clinton enjoys even now, despite his history! Only a charismatic figure who continues to do so much good in the world, could have pulled this off!

His successor, President Bush and his wife also set a great example. Whatever their critics may say about them professionally, one cannot but acknowledge that they have been terrific parents.

Parents need to be very sensitive and listen to their children. Being a parent does not give you the right to yell at them or verbally abuse them.

Listen, listen, listen.

PERSONAL REFLECTION AND DISCUSSION BETWEEN PARTNERS

Q: How good a listener am I? What will my partner say?

A: _____

_____

Q: Do I believe that listening is at the heart of communication in any marriage or relationship?

A: _____

_____

Q: How do my partner and I communicate?

A: _____

_____

Q: Do I feel I know my partner so well that I can finish his or her sentences?

A: _____

_____

Q: Am I ready with a response even before he or she finishes a sentence?

A: _____

_____

Q: Do I listen with my head, ears or heart?

A: _____

_____

Q: Do I know what it means to listen with my heart?

A: _____

Q: Do I listen to only the words of my partner?

A: _____

_____

Q: Do I often say, "I know you" and cut my partner off?

A: _____

_____

Q: Am I interested in listening to my partner?

A: _____

_____

Q: Do I know how to listen to what is not said?

A: _____

_____

Q: What five things within me will I begin to change today to improve my listening skills?

A: _____

Q: Do we spend time alone together to only listen to each other?

A: _____

_____

RULE EIGHT:
Beyond the Village

Former New York Senator and now US Secretary of State, Hillary Rodham Clinton, was once described by the late Richard Nixon, and so many American luminaries, as one of the most remarkable and accomplished women of her generation. She truly is an exceptional person, and like the rest of us, a flawed human being, who in 2007, announced that she will seek the Presidency of the most powerful nation on earth. Her bestseller, *It Takes a Village*, is a remarkable and very thought provoking book on what it takes to raise a child.

I believe that one of the reasons for the 50%+ rate of divorce in the US and the increasingly alarming rate globally is that divorce has become easy. Professional help is not mandatory, it is only an option. In a US court of law, all that matters are "irreconcilable differences." Our extended families have either taken a back seat, or abandoned any and all responsibility. Just as it takes a village to raise a child, it takes the entire family and community, to ensure that a marriage does not end up in divorce court.

Cathy and Robert were married for sixteen years. They were from two different parts of the global village. Cathy was from Chile and Robert from Malaysia. They had two beautiful children. Robert came from a family of stature. Most of the members of his family were professionals in their respective fields. Cathy came from a lower middle class family. They were both beautiful human beings. Nevertheless, Cathy gradually destroyed almost all of her relationships with the people who mattered most; her husband, their children, and many who were close to her.

When the marriage was heading for divorce, and the children were only minors, Roberts's family took a back seat and refused to get involved. This broke Robert's heart. He had done everything within his power, from therapy to church sponsored marriage retreats, to save his marriage. Robert believed that if his family had stepped in, and taken some initiative, his marriage could have been saved.

Elsewhere in this book I have said that the greatest sin in the world is the sin of pride and indifference. No matter how great we are in the eyes of our communities, how religious we are and how often we go to a place of worship, if we do not get involved in the lives of our immediate and larger family, especially during times of crisis, we have accomplished nothing. We will be accountable for what we fail to do.

Life is not a popularity contest. There is a lot to be learned from cultures in which the extended family plays a critical role. The entire society, community and family have a stake in a marriage. It takes more than a village. The great anthropologist, Margaret Mead said, "As a family goes, so goes a nation."

When marriage partners are caught up in the ugliness, heat and passion of battle, they often cease to be rational. The worst in them comes out. Often they cannot tell the forest from the trees. Who better to step in than the people who love them the most and have a stake in the marriage? This is especially critical when there are innocent children involved. Because the families often refuse to or are unable to step in, a therapist enters the stage.

I believe that we are all accountable, no matter how much we rationalize it, if we do not get involved in the marriages in our families. It takes more than a village to preserve a marriage and family. There is no greater task. A great spiritual teacher directed the bulk of his wrath at the people who sat on the sidelines, criticizing, judging, showing the world how great they were and refusing to get involved in the lives of others who desperately needed help, especially those closest to them.

The preservation and celebration of marriage demand that we go beyond the village. We all have a stake in every marriage. Let us begin with our own and those in our families. Let us also encourage those we love, who are in crisis or in marriages that can be so much better, to take advantage of the marriage encounter and family enrichment programs. We have nothing to lose. We have so much to gain.

PERSONAL REFLECTION AND DISCUSSION BETWEEN PARTNERS

Q: What role does my extended family play in our marriage? Is this healthy?

A: _____

_____

Q: Do I want my parents to be a part of our marriage?

A: _____

_____

Q: What relationship do I have with my partner's parents and family? Is this causing a strain or conflict in our marriage or is it helpful?

A: _____

_____

Q: If our relationship is in trouble, are my parents and family playing a positive role? Do I want them to play a role?

A: _____

_____

Q: If our relationship is in trouble, who do I turn to for help?

A: _____

_____

Q: Do I want religious leaders to step in and be supportive? If yes, are they?

A: _____

_____

Q: Do I feel alone in my marriage and unable to talk to anyone? If yes, Why?

A: _____

_____

Q: Am I able to reach out to others close to me for help? If no, why not? And what am I willing to do to make this happen?

A: _____

RULE NINE:
What Music Can Teach Us

Music, in any culture, along with our common humanity, binds all of us together. We laugh to it, weep to it and are deeply moved by it. Most music is dedicated to and born out of love. Let us listen to some of the words that have been put to music:

<u>"I Believe I Can Fly" by R. Kelly</u>

I was on the verge of breaking down,
sometimes silence can be so loud:
there are miracles in life I must achieve:
but first I know it starts inside of me....
I believe I can fly,
I believe I can touch the sky."

<u>"Because You Loved Me" by Celine Dion</u>

For all those times you stood by me
For all the truth that you made me see
For all the joy you brought to my life
For all the wrong that you made right
For every dream you made come true
For all the love I found in you

I'll be forever thankful baby
You're the one who held me up
Never let me fall
You're the one who saw me through, through it all.
You were my strength when I was weak
You were my voice, when I couldn't speak
You were my eyes when I couldn't see
You saw the best there was in me...
I'm grateful for each day you gave me...
I'm everything I am,
because you loved me

"Wind Beneath My Wings" by Bette Midler:

...you are the wind beneath my wings

"The Living Years" by Mike Rutherford

It's too late when we die
too bad we don't see eye to eye
I wasn't there that morning,
when my father passed away:
I wish I could have told him,
all the things I had to say

Our often foolish search for "greener pastures," in another marriage, was best described by Vanessa   Williams in "Save the Best for Last."

Sometimes the very thing you're looking for,

is the one thing you can't see...

"Hero" by Mariah Carey

When you see that hope is gone,

look inside you and be strong

and you'll finally see the truth:

that the hero lies in you

From *Dead Man Walking*:

Be not afraid,

I go before you always,

come follow me

And I will give you rest

Oh, what fools we are!   There is so much we can enjoy and celebrate in the dance of marriage and life.   It can and must be a tango that never ends.

Here are verses from arguably two of the most popular songs sung at weddings these days.   Perhaps, there is something we can learn from them:

"The Rose" by Bette Midler:

Some say love
It is a river
That drowns the tender reed

Some say love
It is a razor
That leaves your soul to bleed

Some say love
It is a hunger
An endless aching need

I say love
It is a flower
And you, it's only seed

It's the heart
Afraid of breaking
That never learns to dance

It's a dream
Afraid of waking
That never takes a chance

It's the one, who won't be taken

Who cannot seem to give

And the soul afraid of dying

That never learns to live

When the night has been too lonely

And the road has been too long

And you think that love is only

For the lucky and the strong

Just remember in the winter

Far beneath the bitter snows

Lies the seed that with the sun's love,

in the spring becomes a rose

"You Raise Me Up" by Josh Groban

When I am down, and oh my soul so weary

When troubles come, and my heart burdened be

Then I am still and wait here in silence

Until you come and sit awhile with me

You raise me up

So I can stand on mountains

You raise me up to walk on stormy seas

I am strong when I am on your shoulders

You raise me up to more than I can be

RULE TEN:
A Lesson From the World of Management

Chances are that almost every person reading this book is touched by the world of management, be it government, a large or small company, a school, village store or any enterprise with two or more people striving to attain a common purpose.

Almost every CEO or Chairman of an organization spouts out the same tune:

"The most important asset we have is our people."

How many of them really believe and live it? The few that do are consistently ranked among the most admired companies in the USA and the world. They practice what they preach. What does this have to do with marriage and relationships? Everything.

What makes an enduring marriage or relationship? I have had the opportunity to address numerous corporate audiences worldwide, and taught and consulted with so many terrific managers at every level. One message to people who run organizations is to be very careful about the kind of people they let through their door.

In other words, the recruitment process is perhaps the most critical challenge that every organization faces. Strategies are absolutely useless unless organizations have the best people to execute them.

The greatest of strategies have failed for one simple reason: poor or no execution.

What is even a greater challenge facing a board of directors is the challenge of hiring the right CEO or the organization's leader. This continues to be the subject of much research among the greatest minds in the world of business and academia.

The choice of a life partner is probably the most important and life changing decision that any free human being can make. Life and death decisions made every second somewhere in the world are an exception. Just as we saw in the world of organizations, the reader is advised to be very careful as to whom he or she "hires" for the job of "life partner." What can we learn from the world of organizations?

I personally spend a great deal of time, developing the corporate culture for organizations, who want it. In some countries, this is resisted, but given the survival rate of organizations and global hyper competition, the organizations who resist this, feel compelled to reconsider their positions.

What is corporate culture? Simply put, it is a living statement of values and beliefs that must govern every aspect of their corporate behavior with all their stakeholders; employees, customers, shareholders, suppliers and society.

Organizational culture must be lived and experienced every moment by every stakeholder. Organizations that have the right organizational culture stand the test of time and are most admired and profitable.

The right organizational culture must be in place before the best and right people are hired. In the interview and recruitment process, each applicant must be made fully aware of the organization's culture and it is the job of the interviewer to determine if the applicant is compatible with the organization's culture and whether he/she will add value.

The choice of a life partner is no different. Living and making a life together is hard enough for the best of people. It is absolutely critical that both partners and their families, find out everything they can about the values, beliefs and dreams of the persons about to make the decision.

They must go through "the recruitment process" before marriage. They must answer and reflect on the several questions found in earlier chapters of this book.

Hopefully the reader will see the connection between the world of business and organizations, and the world of marriage. Perhaps step ten should have been step one!

The Problem with Religion

Prayer and healing services are filled with people who are "looking for a miracle" in a miserable and almost broken marriage between two people of the same faith! It does not matter whether one is a Christian, Buddhist, Hindu, Muslim or of any other faith or even if a person professes to believe "in nothing". I have found throughout the world, that deep down inside, every human being wants to believe in something, "a greater force". In many countries, even non-Christians flock to hear Christian evangelical preachers and healers. They are desperately looking for a miracle and healing.

One or both partners in a marriage relationship may have serious emotional or psychological problems that must be addressed and dealt with, which will be a very painful, yet a liberating experience. Nothing can take the place of psychotherapy, intense marriage counseling or even medication if and when needed. True, spiritual healing has its place.

In the Christian context, confession must not stop with God or a priest. This is an escape route. It does not take much courage to confess our sins or failures to "God" or a priest. Sin, simply put, is a breakdown in the relationship between two individuals when we have done a terrible wrong to another. When we wrong or hurt our partner or another human being, we offend the very heart of humanity.

Having lived in the shadow of Hollywood for over 20 years and being a fan of good movies, I thoroughly enjoyed the film *Blood Diamond*.

In one powerful scene, the lead character played by Leonardo DiCaprio, makes this observation: "Sometimes I wonder if God will ever forgive us for the terrible things we do to each other".

Confession must be made between two individuals. This takes real courage. Pride, self-righteousness and arrogance get in the way. Deep humility is required.

One has control only over oneself. A couple must learn what it is to be a couple. Blame cannot be placed on another. This gets us nowhere. As in the tango, we should start the dance with deep humility. One partner must have the courage to look into the other's eyes and ask the question with humility: "Shall we dance?" Both must be willing to dance as a couple. One cannot dance the tango without each surrendering to the other.

"Religion," observed Karl Marx, "is the opium of the people." It cannot and must not be. It is the greatest liberating force in the world and must make us "fully human and fully alive".

Why do people all over the world flock to charismatic and healing services that make them "feel good" about themselves?

It becomes a drug and a very unhealthy addiction. They "must have the fix". Faith is not just about feeling good. It is about confronting the inner demons within oneself and returning to our homes and workplaces and loving and forgiving those who have hurt us or whom we have hurt or wronged.

A person I know who has an excellent relationship with her eighty six year old bitter and angry mother-in-law blew up and withdrew from the relationship. She buried herself in "her understanding" of her faith, refusing to ask for forgiveness and be totally reconciled with the older lady.

Her "faith" was twisted. When belief and faith are twisted or interpreted to rationalize and justify our own actions, further conflict results. True spirituality demands that we love and forgive those who we hurt and those who hurt us unconditionally.

The instruction is very clear. We must continue to bless those who persecute us. It takes courage to do this. Faith and spirituality, not religion, demands hard work within our inner selves. Gandhi understood this and lived it.

Faith is very hard, but it also demands that each of us "let go of our inner selves", our pride, self-justification and self-righteousness, and become like "a little child". Religion can often be an opiate.. Faith and spirituality must not.

On a global scale, when faith is twisted or misinterpreted to suit our own needs, great crimes against humanity, are committed.

In almost every conflict in our homes, workplaces, families and within and between nations, each of us desperately wants "God" to be on our side!

I hope you can see the huge distinction between religion and spirituality. Religion has, throughout history, been at the root of some of the greatest crimes against humanity. Many wars have been started in the name of religion and still continue.

Spirituality, on the other hand, is based on deep humility, a total trust in a Higher Being or life force, compassion, unconditional love, tolerance and above all forgiveness and reconciliation. This is the heart of all faiths. When any of this is missing, conflict within families, between married partners, within organizations and between nations, occur.

I am often reminded of the words of the great Archbishop of El Salvador, Oscar Romero. He was trying to bring about reconciliation between "the Marxist rebels", the government and the Church. "If we had only known this revolutionary Jesus of the Gospels", they confessed to him, "We would never have become Marxists". The same could be said of Lord Buddha, Mohammed or any other spiritual Master. They were all peacemakers.

Consider the following observations from some of the world's spiritual masters:

"The sufferings of and miseries of men continue because of their neglect of the law of the golden rule given to them two thousand and more years ago." – Leo Tolstoy

"He who loves his fellow man is serving God in the holiest way he can." – Confucius

"Let us live happily without enemies in a world of enmity; let us dwell without enmity among men who are filled with enmity." – The Dhammapada.

" So if you are offering your gift at the altar, and there remember that your brother has something against you, leave your gift there before the altar and go; first be reconciled to your brother, and then come and offer your gift." – Jesus Christ

"There are many religions, but there is only one morality." – John Ruskin

What is the lesson in all of this? At whatever age, the majority of human beings carry a lot of negative and often destructive emotional baggage in relationships or a marriage while continuing their journey of life. A deep spirituality grounded in humility (not religion), can be a powerful help in dealing with this.

We must also be humble enough to seek professional help. We seek professional help for almost everything else in our lives from physicians, lawyers, consultants and teachers. Why don't we seek help for the most important relationship in our lives?

The stigma of seeking professional help to heal a broken relationship or to make it better, must be broken in certain countries. But above all, one must begin a true and deep dialogue with the other partner in the relationship. Both must want to be healed, to grow as a couple, and begin or continue the dance of life together.

The choice is clear. As Sir Elton John, so eloquently put it in his mega hit, "The Circle of Life":

Some of us fall by the wayside;

some of us soar to the stars;

some of us sail through our troubles;

some have to live with the scars"

PERSONAL REFLECTION AND DISCUSSION
BETWEEN PARTNERS

Q: What are we prepared and willing to do as individual human beings and as a couple?

A: _____

_____

Q: What does my faith mean to me?

A: _____

_____

Q: If I am a Roman Catholic, how do I view Evangelical Protestants?

A: _____

_____

Q: If I am an Evangelical Protestant, how do I see Roman Catholics? Do I believe that they are wrong and must be shown the "right path" as I see it or according to my interpretation of the Bible?

A: _____

_____

Q: Do I know the difference between religion, spirituality and faith? If yes, what is it?

A: _____

_____

Q: Based on this, am I religious, spiritual or a person of faith?

A: _____

_____

Q: Do I hide behind my religion? Am I burying myself in my religion to avoid confronting and resolving very real issues that may separate me from my spouse, parents, children and those closest to me?

A: _____

_____

Q: Am I running to Bible Studies, novenas, prayer meetings, rosaries and other "religious" activities? Why?

A: _____

_____

Q: At this point in the book, am I joyful person? Do I know the difference between joy and happiness?

A: _____

_____

Q: Has my faith set me free internally? Am I truly free within to truly express myself?

A: _____

_____

Q: Do I have resentment, anger and fear or any of these towards my spouse, parents, brothers, sisters and others in my life?

A: _____

_____

Q: Has my faith made me a self-righteous and/or proud person? Do I think I am better than others?

A: _____

_____

Q: Are my spouse and I of different faiths? If yes, does this affect our relationship? How?

A: _____

_____

Q: Do I speak ill of others? Why? What am I willing to do to correct this?

A: _____

_____

Q: Am I constantly sitting in judgment of others? Why? What am I willing to do to stop this and live the words of the Master: "Judge not lest you be judged'?

A: _____

_____

Q: Am I constantly looking at the speck in another person's eyes and not in mine? What will I do today to focus totally on the specks in my eye?

A: _____

_____

Q: Am I able to see the best in another human being especially those closest to me? If not, why? What will I do today to change this attitude?

A: _____

_____

Q: What am I willing to do from today to focus on the good in those closest to me and to bring out the best in them?

A: _____

_____

Q: Am I able to forgive myself for doing wrong against others? For disappointing myself?

A: _____

_____

Q: Am I able to forgive others in my life for hurting me and doing wrong against me?

A: _____

_____

Q: How difficult is it for me to say three simple words, "I am sorry", to my spouse and others who I have hurt or wronged? If this is difficult, why? How will I change this?

A: _____

_____

Q: Am I able to have a "conversation with God", but not a conversation with my spouse or those very close to me?

A: _____

_____

Q: What would "God" tell me to do to improve my relationship with my spouse and those close to me?

A: _____

_____

Q: Does my spouse, or those close to me, see "God" within me?

A: _____

_____

Q: Do my colleagues at work and all who come in contact with me see "God" in me?

A: _____

_____

Q: Do I run from church to church simply to make me feel good about myself?

A: _____

_____

Q: Do I only love those who love me?

A: _____

_____

Q: How do I treat others I am not comfortable with or people I dislike or people who dislike me?

A: _____

_____

Q: If married, are my spouse and I able to pray together?

A: _____

_____

Q: Do I accept the fact that my spouse and I are two very different persons?

A: _____

_____

Q: Am I trying to make my spouse what I want him or her to be?

A: _____

_____

Q: Do my spouse and I do everything possible, however uncomfortable, to help each other through crises and very difficult times?

A: _____

_____

Q: Do I constantly attack my spouse or do we always build each other up?

A: _____

_____

Q: Do I stand by my spouse and defend him/her if he/she is wrongly attacked or accused?

A: _____

_____

Q: Do I stand up when I see another person I know being wrongfully attacked or accused or whose reputation is being damaged? Do I do what a "Good Samaritan" is called to do?

A: _____

_____

Q: Do I always justify my behavior?

A: _____

_____

Q: If I have been hurt in a previous marriage or marriages, have I let go of the past and learned to love again? Am I now able to totally love and trust a new marital partner? If no, what am I willing to do today to learn to love and trust again? To avoid this, have I buried myself in my "religion"?

A: _____

_____

Q: What am I willing to do, beginning today, to grow spiritually as a person, and as a couple, with my spouse?

A: _____

_____

Q: Is it more important for me to be a good person or a devout follower of my faith? Do I know the difference? "We all have sinned and fallen short of the glory of God...there is none right-eous, not one."

A: _____

_____

Sex in Marriage

I am deliberately not addressing this topic as a step in improving a relationship between marriage partners. Why? Because in many countries and cultures, sex in marriage is a taboo subject. People, especially partners in a marriage, are not comfortable talking about it or addressing it. In many developing nations where 80% of the human race lives, sex is simply repressed, buried, or when needed is considered a "duty" by marital partners, especially women, and most often, not viewed as something to be mutually enjoyed. I have had many discussions with married partners, mental health professionals and psychiatrists on this topic in these cultures. The distinction between having sex and making love is not often seen especially in rural areas. In many languages, there is really no exact translation for the words "making love". The ordinary people simply cannot relate to it.

Given the impact of television, videos and foreign magazines, people in both rural areas and metropolitan areas are aware of what it means to "be sexy". It remains a curiosity, the way people in other societies, especially women in the West, dress and behave. Many people see the sexiest of movies and celebrities!

In India, teledramas or soap opera are watched even in the most remote areas where a television set is available. Women in rural areas in India and South Asia simply adore the gorgeous Indian actresses and handsome Indian male actors. Indian mega stars like Shah Rukh Khan and Aishwarya Rai have achieved demi-god status. Their movements on the screen are seen as very sexy, even though sex does not occur on the screen. What people see remain in their thoughts and minds.

Sexuality is not taught in schools, and when it is, it is covered in high school as a course on human biology when a child is around sixteen. But there is little or no discussion on how sexuality is to be expressed especially in a marriage. Young girls are taught how to cook and be "good wives". Duty and obedience toward a husband is stressed. Sex and "making love" is ignored.

In many poverty stricken nations, an increasing percentage of mothers seek employment as migrant and domestic workers abroad. When mothers are absent, young unmarried girls are introduced to sex by their fathers and brothers, resulting in very sick incestuous relationships. Some girls are so traumatized by this and other illicit sexual relationships before marriage, that they enter marriage terrified or very uncomfortable with a proper or lawful sexual relationship with a spouse. The honeymoon night can be so very traumatic to many girls and yes, even the young men, when high expectations are not met and for other reasons. After marriage, these girls often show up at the very limited sexual therapy or marriage counseling sessions with their spouses and don't utter a word. Sex to these young girls is perceived as painful and often disgusting. However there are exceptions.

In orthodox or conservative cultures, what happens when the husband discovers the night of the honeymoon, that his wife is not a virgin? He can either accept the situation and continue enjoying "making love" to his new wife, reject her and suffer in silence, or react with violence or verbal abuse. Does he begin to disrespect her after this discovery? If yes, what kind of a life will she have? How do the couples parents react if after a few years, no children are produced? On the other hand, does a pregnancy really satisfy the expectations of mother-in-laws or the parents of both partners? Are children the only real measure of marital success? What really goes on in the bedrooms of spouses in all countries, be it town, village or city? Extended families play a critical role in many cultures.

I have said earlier in the book that "the choices we make dictate the life we live". It is my hope that this book will help each partner in a marriage and those contemplating marriage, make the right choices. We all have only one life to live in this world. I also believe that the choices we make are deeply personal and only the individual can make them. Often right and wrong must be taught at an early age so that the right choices can be made. Ignorance can have devastating personal and social consequences.

One counselor in a major metropolitan mental health center in South Asia revealed to me that the two major reasons for couples coming to her for help were depression and illicit affairs. There are no statistics in many countries. Sex, a very powerful force in human relationships between the sexes, is often repressed.

The workplace, where working people spend the bulk of their lives, provides the most convenient and fertile ground for extra-marital affairs. Employees spend more time with their colleagues than with their own spouses! Emotional support that they may not be getting at home can be provided by a colleague of the opposite sex and this can also lead to an illicit sexual relationship.

What about sexual harassment in the workplace and even in public transportation? How many are reported around world?

What about men? Listen to the many conversations between men about sex in "macho" cultures. Women are often seen as sexual objects. The conversations center on sexual conquests and women are often described in sexual terms. There is little respect between the sexes when it comes to sexuality. Healthy and respectful conversations on sexuality are rare among men, especially in these male dominated societies.

If a wife does not satisfy the sexual needs of her husband, he simple turns elsewhere. The first one to feel the existence of another lover is the wife. Denial can also play a role. Societies in many cultures have told most of them to suffer in silence. Among the rich and even the middle class, where children and comforts are provided to the woman by the husband, they simply tolerate and exist with the "other woman". Sometimes, the husband knows that the wife has a lover. This can result in rage, domestic violence, and even suicide or murder. Men and women handle extra marital affairs very differently. For this, there are no statistics in many parts of the world. In a silent society, no one reports any illicit sexual incident or crime. Shame is the driving force and life simply must go on.

Many partners run to religion to hear day after day, week after week, that "God loves them". They have a desperate need to feel and believe that there is nothing wrong with them. The problem is never resolved. It is simply buried or denied in a warped perception of religion as we saw in the previous chapter. In so many societies, this denial, begins after the children are born (after the marital duty is performed) and goes on for decades till death.

In a marriage, when one partner or both constantly snap at each other or really don't respect each other, how can sex between them be really enjoyed? Can they ever truly make love? How many bedrooms are there in the world where sex is seen as a duty to be discharged? How many couples are there who co-exist because of children, family, cultural and social reasons? The charade or show simply must go on. Do marital partners treat each other the same way in their bedrooms, homes and in social settings? The immortal words of Shakespeare ring true: "Above all, to thine own self be true."

I am also told that in compact houses or dwellings in rural societies where they have very thin walls, women are terrified or ashamed to have sex with their partners, because a neighbor could be listening! There are so many such dwellings in poor nations.

In many cultures, bisexuality and homosexuality are common. In small cities, towns and villages all over the world, there really are no secrets. When known, these situations are either dismissed with humor, or such people are shunned. Nothing is confronted or resolved. There are arranged marriages of the powerful, wealthy and connected, where sexual compatibility is not addressed or is not even an issue. This also happens among the poor and middle class.

What emerges is a very sick and perverted sexual society. Making love is a beautiful thing. It was given to us by the creator to enjoy between married partners. Society, churches and other spiritual leaders must address this issue. Making love and a healthy sexual relationship between partners also results in better self-esteem, emotional and physical health. It has tremendous medical benefits, according to clinical research published in more advanced countries.

It is ironic, that along with unbelievable sexual repression in many cultures, there exists is an equally unbelievable amount of sexual freedom, especially among the rich and middle class. Long weekends are celebrated by those who can afford it, with different sexual partners, alcohol and even narcotics. Beach resorts in Indonesia, Thailand, Sri Lanka, Mexico and the Caribbean, have become a paradise for this frolicking and bohemian behavior.

There is so much more that can be written on this subject by mental health professionals who are actually in the trenches listening to marriage partners. I hope this book either begins or advances the discussion.

Let me make one thing clear. There are many marriages in which the partners are totally fulfilled with each other, both sexually and emotionally. In other marriages, partners admit to problems or challenges and both are committed to resolving differences and satisfying each other sexually and emotionally in a monogamous relationship.

What can individuals in a marital relationship and those intending to get married do, to have a mutually satisfying and monogamous sexual relationship? I realize that my suggestions may be contrary to the thinking in most societies! A revolution in sexuality may be the answer.

- Each partner should be aware of each other's sexuality and sexual needs before marriage. Is this possible in different cultures? I think it is, but it demands a radical change in mindset.

- Each partner should make sure there is sexual compatibility between them before marriage.

- Children should be taught at an early age about the sanctity and beauty of sexuality. This is the responsibility primarily of parents. Schools, churches, temples and mosques can also play a critical role.

- Children should be taught to make the right choices in life, especially in the choice of a life partner, which is perhaps the most important decision they will ever make.

- Pre-marital counseling should be made mandatory in every society given the social, emotional and even medical costs of "unhappy" marriages. The impact on children of such marriages can be devastating.

- Children live what they learn.

- When children witness sexual discord between parents, which often manifests itself in a lack of respect between their parents or even verbal abuse, they can end up making wrong choices by marrying the wrong partner for the wrong reasons. In some cases, children of such marriages simply find marriage as a way of escape and spend the rest of their lives in regret. This can be avoided.

The Wedding, Marriage & Parenting
By Mrs. Shanthi Wijesinghe

I will never understand why Gerard singled me out to write this section to his wonderful book. It's not as if we've known each other for eons! Is it because I look at life practically? Or because of my work with children and families for over twenty-five years? He refuses to divulge.

When two peas fall heavily for each other and decide to live in the same pod, no one should stand in their way - chemistry does its job!

Our pod with the two little peas has seen major setbacks and disappointments, heartbreak and momentary elation, comic strip scenarios and disastrous endings almost each day! The little peas have indeed grown...*but*, I would probably do it all over again with some major adjustments.

Same man, same kids but not quite the same ME! In fact, not *me* in it at all.

I had a lot of learning and a lot of growing up to do. For starters...my outlook on marriage was very staid. I had rebelled against it from the time I was 18. To me it was the end to independency-doomed for life to slave for another human being who may just end up beating the life out of me if I dared to disagree! For someone like myself, marriage shouldn't be on the list of "things to do"!

But parents being parents and relatives being relatives did their bit and I ended up saying "yes" without thinking – or I was tired of saying "no". This occurs in many cultures.

Oh sure before marriage, there was the adrenaline excitement that men were being fished out from ponds and lakes and wherever else, to have a look at me...felt like a cow in a meat market!

The "left on the shelf" tag is discreditable against parents with girls. As children, we go against our principles and wishes to please our parents no end. It's the worst mistake a parent can make against their child. They believe that they are stamping our future with bounty. That is the furthest from the truth. If all parents are to give their daughters their best, it would be a place to live so that she has a place to call her own.

Men in many male dominated-cultures approach marriage as an investment for themselves. If they think the woman is feisty enough, their investment is assured. They use their wife's boundless energy and financial resources to make themselves comfortable for life. I am all for chipping in but when the chips are demanded aggressively, it leaves a bitter aftertaste. Being submissive, most of us give in, because we want peace at any cost and money is not something we should be debating about at the beginning of a marriage.

What mattered at the time was that we had one thing in common – the love for music. Neil Diamond and Abba – two different planets, but music all the same!

My mother-in-law had 8 (yes, eight) children. She said she never regretted bearing any of them even though she lost one just after six months of his birth. She treasured them all.

Her love was unconditional and self-giving. Each child was special. She did not favor one above the other however much heartache she went through with at least one of them. Truly, a wonderful species of woman.

When my husband proposed marriage I said "" Yeah, ok! But I can't cook!" (What I meant was I wasn't willing to be the good little stay-at-home-housewife and his caregiver but he had understood differently- I wasn't going to correct him either!)

My m-i-l's rejoinder had been: "why do you want to make that an issue? She will learn. If you like her then you should marry her. After all, you cook at home every day and you can both eat from home." Wish there were more like her.

Marriage in many cultures is a fairy tale spun by adults who are hell-bent on getting their children married. Nary is a whisper heard of the groom's penchant for drink, womanizing or homosexuality or the bride's love of extravagance or experimentation of sexual partners. "Oh, that'll all sort itself out after he is married" is a firm favorite among many marriage hunters. "Ah, she'll be ok after she's married" is part of that same mantra.

Realistically speaking, it's all to do with showing off. The bride's people vs. the bridegroom's people. And what a show it turns out to be. Hot damn – grand slam!

What it does to the couple is anyone's guess. Six months down the road or before the first photographs of the wedding have cooled, or the hotel bills settled, the couple is having their major brawl with the neighbors all preening their ears to pass on the tidbits....

"...and then she said...."

"...and you know what he said...."

This is why the aspect of counseling is so important to any two people intending to stay together till the "death do us part" act.

Most mothers in conservative cultures continue to be at fault. They bring up their sons crooning endearments and keeping the wolves at bay. From their early years, boys aren't allowed to fall, scrape themselves, graze their knees and girls aren't allowed into a boy's domain. In fact girls are brought up to weather the toils because "she's going to bear a lot of pain".

With the event of the boy finally "growing up" he wants mothering – not a give-take partnership. He wants to be taken care of, cooked and cleaned for, dried behind the ears, packed and sent off to work to bring home the dough which he surreptitiously peels off to his mother citing various reasons. He makes excuses for her loneliness. He leaves the wife unattended for days and spends his time in his family home. He feels he has to "look after" his married and unmarried sisters (because that's what he's been brought up to understand by his parents) believing and expecting his wife to run their home.

An odd telephone call during the day to check if all is well in his home and he is as happy as a lark to receive the undivided attentions of his mother and clan! After a few days, guilt begins to set in, and of course he is missing the sex....

Women in many cultures are silent sufferers of this weak spot because they want to "'keep the family peace". Others fight for justice and decide to call it a day going on to becoming happier and better placed individuals.

In many cultures, when it comes to the –mother/son bonding, the apron strings hold fast. Mothers tend to hold on to their sons with vice-like grips and at the same time want them to marry in order to produce a bloodline. Many women fall for this hook, line and sinker.

It is sad when parents bring up children to suit their needs.

Let's face it. Kids don't ask to be born. They are placed on earth by us. The responsibility is squarely placed on our shoulders. We have to make choices, many sacrifices and by the time the kids are 11 and 12 our investment on time and energy has paid off. Unfortunately, there isn't enough stress on "the afterwards" because no two people who are going to live under the same roof come with a life-long guarantee to commitment and amendments.

We take the vows in church or before a registrar of marriage, but does a couple really envisage what's in store for them?

Everyone starts off great. By the end of three months many couples have had their first disagreement and most of the time it is because we are trying to shield our parent family.

We argue every case in the book against our spouse's opinion. What we want to do is raise the acceptance level but in fact we do more damage when we argue defiantly for our parents, siblings and relatives. It is absolute suicide!

I learnt the true meaning of "silence is golden" very early on in marriage, but it makes a lot of dents in one's emotional framework. Staying quiet at the time of the verbal attack against your family is the sacrifice one makes in a marriage.

Bedtime can be the greatest soother, because as the author of this book says, sexual intimacy between married partners in many cultures is used to make the emotional pain go away at least for the time being. No verbal communication is needed. One "bottles up" the pent up frustrations for years to come or until death. Before either falls off to sleep you will each be chanting "what a wonderful world"!

The verse below is from an email that has been circulating for some time.

Love is holding hands in the street
Marriage is holding arguments in the street.

Love is dinner for two in your favorite restaurant.
Marriage is a fast food take-out

Love is cuddling on a sofa
Marriage is deciding on a sofa

Love is talking about having children
Marriage is talking about getting away from children

Love is going to bed early
Marriage is going to sleep early

Love is a romantic drive
Marriage is a tarmac drive
Love is losing your appetite
Marriage is losing your figure

Love is sweet nothing in the ear
Marriage is sweet nothing in the bank.

Love is a flickering flame

Marriage is a flickering television

Love is one drink and two straws

Marriage is: "Don't you think you've had enough?"

In short, love is blind.

Marriage is an eye opener!

CASE STUDY 1:

Juanita was going into her twenty-third year of life when she met the most marvelous man on earth (a die-hard Latin American brought up in true Latin style by a doting mother – we all know the type!) and both decided they were made for each other. He was twenty-nine and considered the worthiest bachelor within their circle. Sparks flew instantly and the 'chemistry' was at its height working overtime in both the young lives.

After their first night out they decided there was nothing more to wait for and so began the most glorious six months of planning their wedding and the trappings which go to make an absolute carnival for relatives, friends and colleagues. The bride's parents didn't spare spending precious millions on hotels, wedding finery, jewelry and other extras which turn a simple ceremony of exchanging vows into an orgy for gluttons.

With an extra step in her stride the waiting bride grabbed life with both hands and thanked her God for sending this man her way.

Juan was a decent guy. He was intent on completing his Master's degree which would allow him time for marriage the coming year and wanted very much to lead a contented and happy life with lots of kids around. He was an only child and missed Juanita's companionship and happy family life she was leading with her sisters and brothers.

Life's good !

The first two years were exhilarating. They visited places in their country they thought never existed. They shared poetry and books. Friends and family commented on how good they looked together. One year down the road, the mother-in-law factor began playing a major role in their lives especially because she kept on reminding them that she would like seeing a grandchild (or two) playing in her garden. Then of course there was the case of the property. There weren't many on her side that she would like to donate her lands.

Juanita became pregnant. And then there were four!

Suddenly she found herself in a black pool of depression. The babies followed each other pretty fast. They were adorable and weren't difficult to look after, but, she could not get up on time, make Juan's breakfast and go to work anymore. Not in that order anyhow. She set the alarm for 4am, did the laundry, made breakfast, cooked lunch, washed and cleaned the toilets, ironed and did the hundreds of "little" jobs we all do around our homes every day.

And what of the "man of the house?" Well, he argued he wasn't cutout for the job! In fact the babies were too messy and his woman was looking a little slovenly. Surely, he countered, she could look nice when he got home?

By the time they reached their sixth wedding anniversary, Juanita had had enough and wanted out. She didn't fight. There was nothing to fight about and she couldn't be bothered discussing anything with her husband. She simply filed for divorce. She wanted the kids though, because she felt it was her duty to look after them.

Juan was devastated and infuriated. He blamed Juanita's parents and everyone remotely connected to her for the split. He refused to part with the kids who were by now in a state of confusion. The youngest (two years old) had to be re-introduced to diapers at night and almost half the day. The eldest (a boy) went into non-verbal shock and would only communicate with his preschool teacher.

The crime is against the innocent children parents bring into the world who are torn apart by mixed emotions and trauma which will stay with them for the rest of their lives if timely intervention is not sought.

CASE STUDY 2:

Jenny married her boyfriend Ahmed of eight years, in an elaborate ceremony. They were of different faiths which made friends, relatives and critics give their unasked opinion freely. Ahmed's mother hated Christians for some reason. Jenny suffered silently but with accumulating rage. Ahmed was putty when in his mother's presence. Each morning she would come around to taste the dishes Jenny had prepared. She would then pack a lunch for her son and replace it while no one was looking.

"My son is not used to eating this muck!" was her constant vile comment.

After six years of this abuse, Jenny decided to call it quits. Ahmed didn't fight her. Fortunately there were no children from this union.

CASE STUDY 3:

Roshan and Sharmila lived and worked as professionals in the US, he in Northern California and her in New York City. They were both born in India. Their marriage was decided for them by their parents in India. Sharmila had the longest hair and was blessed with an angelic face. Her voice was of the softest timbre. Unfortunately Roshan was the same. Even a blind person could have seen the missing link in this unusual pair. As Sharmila was not conceiving they decided to adopt a set of twins. All was well for a time, until Sharmila for some unknown reason broke out in dark brown patches from the neck down. They tried everything. Psychologists, counselors, and medical doctors worked on the case overtime. After two years an Ayurvedic doctor in India asked one simple question from Sharmila : "Are you in love again ?"

The story broke in the family circles and there was much heartache. Later, during counseling sessions and therapeutic programs we learned that the marriage had never been consummated. Roshan was simply not interested in sex and Sharmila had fallen in love with another. A year later Sharmila re-married. Her patches cleared up within months and she was her former self again.

Roshan's parents, when contacted, disclosed that they had known of his homosexual tendencies but thought everything would be "ok" after marriage.

In many cultures, there is a high rate of denial when it comes to protecting one's child.

PRESERVING MOTHERHOOD IN MANY CULTURES

Having not being told by card/song/candle-lit dinners that I am considered the world's "No. 1 Mother" after the kids hit the teen years, does not upset me. The way I see things: What's the point of a day's celebration if Mothers who have been serenaded and garlanded have to pick up after their children from the morning after celebrating Mothers' Day ? The fruits of my labor have not been in vain. The 'investment' has paid off. And that's considered a bonus by most in my league.

The Roles of a Mother Include:

- Financial supporter

- Dishwasher and laundry-maid until 11 pm

- Family sounding board and messenger

- Dual role player: bedmate and doormat

- Chauffeur, cook, maid, secretary, coordinator

- Manager in disaster and crisis management

All for the pursuit of raising future leaders! Forget the politicians. This is too much work for them. What I mean by future leaders are children who will be able to:

- Cope with tolerance

- Have good manners

- Able to accept defeat
- Make decisions
- Shoulder responsibility

Teachers with thirty years or more experience say that today's child is, in general, much less respectful and much less courteous than the child of a generation ago. Unless children learn respect for others, beginning with adults at home, they can never learn to respect themselves.

Manners and Respect are Inseparable!

At my school, children who respond to a teacher's call with "Why, Miss Shanthi?" are quietly asked to replace the phrase with: "I'm coming, Miss Shanthi!" It gives them a sense of esteem to say the entire sentence confidently. At home, parents say they use: "I'm coming, Mom!" spontaneously.

Children begin developing respect for others by first developing it for their parents. Children should be taught to behave politely toward their parents. That means children should not be allowed to call their parents (or any adult for that matter) by their first names, (however cute you may think it is), to interrupt adult conversations unless in crisis, or (beyond age three) to throw tantrums when they don't get their way.

When adults speak, children should pay attention; and when adults give instruction, children should carry them out. It's as simple as that.

Developing table manners at home makes you proud parents.

Learning to Enjoy Simple Pleasures

Unlike a generation ago, children are comparing material effects. They are comparing prices and sizing each other up from as young as age six.

De-commercialize. Don't feel obliged to throw expensive birthday parties or theme parties so that you will be accepted into a group. Children must know from a very young age that there are limits and what one person does need not be the best.

Don't use material goods to show your children you love them. When you ask adults about their most treasured childhood memories, they rarely mention the gifts they received. They talk about learning to do things with parents or grandparents – planting a fruit tree in the garden, fixing a chair or making cookies.

Raising Kids with Caring Hearts

Such children are sure to lead successful and happy lives. The latest research suggests parents are not incorporating the critical ingredients necessary to raise kids who are clear about right and wrong. When parents raise single children, they feel that life must rotate around the child. Husband-wife relationships suffer greatly because of this. Undivided attention is a sure way of bringing up a precocious and selfish child in to society.

Nurture Empathy

Every day is an opportunity to teach your child the value of another person's feelings. When your children fight, when they see someone struggling in the world, when parents are tired…these are the countless opportunities to help your child see the world with compassion instead of how it affects them. Without this all-important virtue, all the love in the world will not prevent your child from swaying from peer pressure and the negative influences so widespread today.

Create a Conscience

The alarming rise in the rates of youth violence, peer cruelty, stealing, cheating, promiscuity and substance abuse are indications of this frightening problem. The acts themselves are scary enough. The horrifying part is that most kids do not feel badly that they have behaved in these ways. There is increasing evidence that kids today have no guidelines strong enough to develop the thoughts needed to guide their behavior.

Self-Control

Children need to see this behavior modeled in their daily lives. Modeling self-control is the most critical influence to nurture this trait. Helping your child learn to deal with strong emotions is also a key ingredient to successfully integrating self-control in their personality.

Educating ourselves is the first step to making sure our kids get the information they need to make the right choices and have the lives they deserve.

"Our children are not going to be just "our children" - they are going to be other people's husbands and wives and the parents of our grandchildren." - Mary S. Calderone

"NORMALIZATION" OF PARENTS AND EXTENDED FAMILY

It is astounding to witness the willingness of parents today to accommodate and adjust schedules and structures for children. Adults feel that they should be only too willing to make accommodations for their children even though their behavior is one of irresponsibility and indifference. The result of this is that children often suffer from a "hidden disability" of over-dependency or being spoiled with a sense of "entitlement."

I feel strongly that parents need the strength to first normalize them in order to handle the demands of a growing child.

I used to be a frenzied mom for a very, very short while. Then I discovered my 'tone'. The one used especially for kids to tell them in no uncertain terms that I meant business. It still works!

People tell me that this is because:

a) My kids have the sword of Damocles hanging over their heads

b) They have been well-trained

It's actually a bit of both. It's the classic tit-for-tat phenomenon. If they are nice to me – I am nice in more ways than one but if they want to manipulate me into difficult corners they have to pay for it in numerous ways.

No screaming, shouting or worse – pleading, begging and cajoling on my part to get things done around the house. If the beds were not made I simply closed the door on them. If a mug was lying around I made sure it stayed there until the offender needed it. If a uniform didn't come out of the wash, well, I wasn't the one going to school!

"Why me Lord?"

Outbursts from selfish, rude, and demanding children are symptoms of a rapidly growing epidemic that is spreading among the career-oriented families.

Over-indulgent, extravagant behavior is best referred to as acting like a "spoiled brat". A recent survey we did revealed that 85% of adults think kids today are more spoiled than kids of ten or fifteen years ago. More than 2/3 of parents admit that their own kids are spoiled. Consequently, parents and educators are left wondering why they are faced with this "spoiled brat" crisis and what can be done to kill the back-talk, bossiness and arrogance seen in today's kids.

Highly Contagious Ailment

As parents we are responsible for our children's qualities. If your child is thought to be:

Arrogant	Irresponsible
Bad Tempered	Jealous
Cheater	Judgmental
Cheeky	Bad Mannered
Cruel	Lazy
Demanding	Manipulative
Domineering	Narrow Minded
Greedy	Uncooperative
Impatient	Ungrateful
Insensitive	Unhelpful

It's time to start on the corrective measures NOW!

The Underlying Cause of Bad Attitudes

Kids who see the world as a cold and cruel place are selfish and insensitive. They believe it's acceptable to treat others with malice, disrespect, and intolerance.

Kids with bad-tempered attitudes usually start out by displaying their anger in unhealthy ways, such as biting, hitting, tantrums, or fighting. If not corrected instantly these bad behaviors turn into bad habits, and soon the child develops one big attitude that says to us all, "I'll use my anger to get what I want."

Kids who are insecure, fearful, and anxious may conceal or compensate for their feelings with attitudes of distrust, jealousy, and suspicion. Bad attitudes run deep and can last a lifetime

Parents, who always pick up after their children, make excuses for their child's behavior and completely deny the truth to themselves, face a lifetime of dependency and manipulation. Bad attitudes are the foundation for bad character

Children who have learned how to get away with being irresponsible and uncooperative often end up as adults with a twisted moral angle. Bad attitudes can lead to a lifetime of unhappiness and social isolation

Kids who are spoiled, self-centered, arrogant, and disrespectful will not be able to form lasting attachments or find personal fulfillment.

"What we need to do is look long and hard at our part in all this. Where did our children get the message that the rules don't apply to them? And where did we, the Mothers, get the message that if we abdicate our responsibilities as Mothers, the Universe will do our job for us? And it does, but without any of the love and tenderness and compassion that we could have given, along with the lessons." -- Jamie Lee Curtis, actress

Responsible Fathers Aren't Born – They're Made!

Stereotypes affect parenting style. Mothers have a great role to play in bringing up boys in any country. Spoon feeding is the greatest tragedy committed in the name of love. The conventional family seems to be a concept of the past, with more women now in full time employment. Parents find themselves in the position of splitting parental responsibilities in a number of ways in order to secure personal and individual achievement inside and out of employment.

Men should be more involved in a holistic aspect of their children's lives.

Fathers are either excluded or exclude themselves from becoming involved with children. Mothers initially assume that fathers do not want to be involved as the children get older. Fathers' responsibilities are at times often challenged by way of activity. It is thought that fathers cannot cross over to the softer side, in fear of not living up to the so called "macho" image, and coming across as showing too much of their feminine side.

And do real men cook? Oh yes they do! Or at least they should be taught that cooking is a big part of the home-maker's scene. That it is not 'degrading' to be seen with a spoon in a masculine hand!

So parenting is all about making choices. Not necessary the right ones. We may get duped along the way but hey, everyone makes mistakes.

We just have to learn the best way to handle ourselves and our families. Twenty years from now there's no point regretting.

Good luck!

‖ Marriage, Family & Work Performance

This is a subject of great interest to me. How people behave and act in organizations in different national cultures has been part of my professional, consulting and management education experience for over twenty-five years. The bulk of our lives are spent getting to and from work and at work. This consumes about ten hours or more. Those of us lucky enough to get eight hours of sleep each day, are only left with six hours to enjoy our families and deal with our own personal challenges. The vast majority of people in the US, Europe and in every major city in the world use public transportation to get to and from work. In the post – 9/11 world, with public transportation being blown up now and then, many commuters suffer in silence and hope they reach home alive. What goes on in our homes and families in the US, Europe and so many nations also has a tremendous impact on our performance as employees in organizations. Imagine the impact of this fear, family and marital stress on work performance and the bottom line.

Denial of almost everything has become a way of life in many cultures including Western cultures. "Issues" are rarely or ever addressed till they explode. When they are discussed, often emotions run high. Fear of reprisal in the workplace, fear of what other people think, fear of one another, fear of losing one's job as well as shame, have gripped the workplace. Collectively, all of this has a dramatic effect on an organization's profitability in business and government. True, government is not in the business of making a profit but the most admired and competitive nations are run as a business. A great American once observed: "the business of America is business". Singapore is now Singapore, Inc!

The stress of family life, especially with extended families playing a dominant role in many cultures, takes its toll on performance at work. Keeping a marriage and family together as we have seen throughout this book no matter where we live in the world, is hard work. Single mothers have additional challenges. Individual performance at work has a direct impact on an organization's profitability and survival. In fact, one could argue that it is the primary driver of profitability and growth. Virtually every management guru and CEO tells us that an organization's most valuable asset is its people, talent or human resources. But what do organizations really do to meet the needs of this most valuable asset and get the best out of its people?

I am a Sri Lankan born American. The first ten years of my life were spent in Sri Lanka, then Ceylon. I was a mere infant and a child. Almost ten years of my teenage and young adult life was spent in India. Am I more Indian or Sri Lankan? I went to the US for my graduate studies and have lived and worked there for half my life. My teaching, speaking and professional life has taken me to so many countries on so many continents. As a result of these experiences, I have worked with, taught and counseled individuals, managers and executives from virtually every corner of the world and have some real knowledge of the impact of their personal and family lives on the workplace and their individual work performance.

In his book, "The War over Work – the Future of work and Family", published by Melbourne University Press, 2005, Australian author Don Edgar made these interesting observations:

"Managers are focused on the bottom line and fail to see that profit comes from good performance, which comes from job satisfaction, morale and commitment, and the discretionary effort that a satisfied worker puts in coming from feeling valued as a whole person, not simply a cog in the wheel of production. Managers will say the shareholder or customer must come first, not feeling that unless employees come 'equal first', the whole social system of the workplace comes unstuck and profits go out the door".

The five most commonly mentioned family problems cited:

Time Pressures – 47%

Lack of social and recreational time – 33%

Financial difficulties – 23%

Juggling work-family commitments with the spouse – 17%

Relationship difficulties with the spouse – 15%

The five most commonly mentioned work problems:

Coming home feeling stressed – 53%

Having to change work hours at short notice – 34%

Relationship problems with co-workers – 33%

Coming home late from work – 27%

Pressures from work deadlines – 25%

Management and employees try to separate work from the rest of their lives as if once they enter the workplace the rest of their lives goes away. For most people, this simply does not happen. There must be no doubt in the readers mind that many employees have a difficult time balancing family responsibilities and their own individual fears, anxieties and struggles with the demands of the workplace.

The sad reality is that in several nations, so many people spend their entire lives in jobs that they should not have been in, in the first place. Organizations are ill-served and the individual employee suffers in silence not becoming "all or more than he or she can be". The sadder reality is that most of these lovely souls are not even aware of this. They settle for so much less and the result is that when they go home unfulfilled and sad, they remain depressed and are not able to really enjoy their families. Some do this for thirty-five years or more! The family/work/life challenge works both ways. The problem can be in the home or the workplace or both. Every human being, deep inside, longs for meaning, purpose, to be valued, to love and be loved.

Psychiatrists and psychologists who have researched the holocaust in Germany and inmates in the worst prisons in the world, discovered this. There really are no exceptions. It is what each of us settles for in life. There are few things sadder than a wasted life. Each of us is born into this world with some talent.

The words in the beautiful song "Something Good" in the film *Sound of Music* has a lesson for us. "Nothing comes from nothing; nothing ever could; for somewhere in my youth or childhood, I must have done something good."There is good in every human being.

The most admired and profitable organizations in the world have realized that happy and satisfied employees are the primary driver of sustained profitability. Only happy, satisfied and valued employees can create real and sustained shareholder value and customer delight that lasts. These organizations create internal corporate cultures that address the very real struggles in each employee's personal and family life that are an obstacle to maximum individual performance, morale, loyalty and commitment, all of which lead to maximum profits.

The war is no longer merely over work. In today's new global knowledge economy, the real war is the "war to find and keep the best talent". Organizations must identify and address the challenges and stresses that keep their best people from performing to their fullest. Women are a driving force in the new economy. Many of them are faced with the challenges of being a single mother. Employers must embrace and address these challenges and do whatever it takes to retain their best people, especially their best women.

QUESTION FOR EVERY READER

Q: What I am going to do with the rest of my life? Do I want to become all that I can be? Do I even understand what this means? Do I care?

A: _____

_____

QUESTIONS FOR EVERY EMPLOYER

Q: What are we doing today to satisfy the very critical personal, professional and family needs of our people (our most valuable asset?) which affect individual and company performance and profitability?

A: _____

_____

Q: How are we addressing the very real challenges faced by our employees, especially the best, who may be experiencing serious problems in their marriage? In their home?

A: _____

_____

Q: What are we doing today to address the challenge of childcare faced by our people? Other challenges faced by married and single mothers?

A: _____

_____

Q: What will we begin doing tomorrow?

A: _____

Q: What are we doing to recruit, develop and retain the best talent?

A: _____

Case Studies – Real Stories: Should We Be Taking Baggage to Our Graves?

It is absolutely amazing and so very distressing to see people reach the age of fifty, sixty, seventy and even eighty-five with so much emotional baggage, hurt, anger, resentment, jealousy and the inability to forgive themselves and others.

MARIA

Born in Colombia, South America Maria now lives in Los Angeles. She's 64. Every time I see her react to certain situations and the show she puts on for everyone, I am reminded of the Paul McCartney song: "When I'm 64"! Even Sir Paul did not realize when he first wrote the song, that he would be going through a very public and ugly divorce when he turned 64!

Getting back to Maria, in the presence of others, she is constantly on stage. She is an excellent performer. The relationship between her, her siblings and her mother has fallen apart. She is however a devout Catholic with unwavering devotion to the Blessed Virgin Mary. She knows and sees the severe trauma within the family, but refuses to confront and help resolve it. When asked why, she responds: "You know me. I want peace at any cost." Life to her is all about public relations. To the outside world, she appears to have a good marriage. I don't know what her husband really thinks of her. I know the husband is completed dominated by her. He is in his 70s! Maria is also very guarded about the lives of her children. The show goes on, on a global stage.

There are people like Maria who believe that they should mind their own business, ignore wrong, injustice and crimes within the family, and have "peace at any cost". To Maria, the popularity contest must be won. It was the great Martin Luther King who said: "what we remember is not the words of our enemies, but the silence of our friends (and family members)".

Maria's mother is old. Most of her peers are dead. While visiting her mother in Colombia, she spotted a valuable wooden carving which she wanted to take with her. The mother had forgotten that she had earmarked this same carving for one of her sons. Maria resented this at the age of 64 and told her brother: "Mum said I could have it." A day before Maria left Colombia for the US, her brother told her that she could have the carving. Maria replied on the phone: "If I take it now, I will get mad every time I see it!" This was an infantile response! Where does all this negative behavior or baggage come from? Do Maria's numerous fans all over the world where she performs know this part of her or is this part closely guarded?

Do we take these resentments, anger and other negative emotions to our graves? Can we not forgive ourselves and each other, and work tirelessly for reconciliation especially within our own families? Does any amount of devotion to a Higher Being matter if we do not resolve all anger, hatred, jealousy and resentment before we reach our graves?

CATHY

Cathy just turned 49. She lives in Maryland and is in her second marriage because of an earlier physically abusive relationship. She has never faced or dealt with anything in her life. Her first husband, two children and her parents lived under the same roof. Her parents were in one unit and she and her family in the other. When she walked out of her marriage, she simply walked in to her parent's unit with her children and was "taken care of".

She has never known what most divorced women with children have known all over the world; what it means to live alone as a single mother. She was Catholic. But the Catholic Church turned a blind eye to her at the time of her greatest need. Along came the evangelicals who excel in "taking a person in", comforted her and met her very urgent needs.

She then buried herself in "born again" religion and never really confronted herself. The Catholic Church lost her. She continued with her profession every day and had her children jointly raised with her parents. Several years later, a man entered her life and they married.

In her second marriage, Cathy is unable to sit down and have a real conversation with her new husband.

A very close friend, Laura and her husband Michael, who has a substance abuse and diagnosed psychological problem, have leaned on Cathy for emotional support their entire married life. As a result of this, Cathy has completely buried her problem with her husband, and devoted much of her energy to listening for hours to Michael, even when he is in the worst stupor, babbling and incoherent, without taking immediate action to do what had to be done. Laura and her husband are also very close to Cathy's husband who has repeatedly told her not to pamper Michael and to cut off the lengthy phone conversations, and get him into treatment. In his mind, Michael had wrongly believed that his wife Laura had engaged in a long extramarital affair with a member of his own family.

Cathy's own marriage was suffering. She sought help from various churches. She spoke to the clergy about Michael in the hope of finding help for that family.

She did not sit down with her own husband who was longing to have a conversation with her. She read several self-help and religious books, including *Conversations with God*, but was unable to have a conversation with her own husband.

Cathy had two adult children who harbored much anger toward her for leaving their father, her first husband. One of the children finally dealt with this and is now married to a fine young man. The other child still remains a problem. He struggles with substance abuse and much anger toward his mother. Cathy's new husband has done what he can for her two children.

His own two children from a previous marriage live overseas. Cathy did not seem to care. Cathy insists that Michael and Laura need her more. She has not come to terms with the reality that they are only good friends and not her immediate family.

She had not come to terms with the reality that her first priority nowwere her new husband, her children and her new husband's children.

There are so many people I have encountered all over the world like Cathy, who solve the problems of others, without first addressing their own. Cathy must understand and accept the reality that she must focus on dealing with the mutual anger between herself and her son. She must give first priority to restore and build the relationship between herself and her new husband.

She has no idea what it means to be a couple. Together, she and her new husband can accomplish much. If she only turns to him and says: "How can I help you and how can we together build our marriage?" the situation can be sorted out.

Cathy's new husband knows her potential but she is unable to comprehend this. She has always been in bondage and is surrounded by people who do not challenge her. She is threatened by and uncomfortable, though cordial, with women who are smart, ambitious, have a desire to learn new things, and stretch themselves to grow. A person is known by the company he or she keeps. The company Cathy keeps is pretty dismal. They remain in their comfort zones. Her new husband tries to get her to see a new world. She fights him. The only way Cathy can enter this new world is by taking a painful and long journey into the depths of her heart and soul.

There are so many partners who have been so gradually traumatized, that they do not even know how dysfunctional they have become. They are unable to love and be loved. Even when they love, it is not a healthy and unconditional love. It says: "I will love only if...".

Unconditional love frees the lover and the loved. Both can be who they are. Unconditional acceptance liberates.

GEORGE

I have spent so much time with George. He is very tragic. He is almost 80 years old and has been married to the same woman for over 50 years. It is a marriage that should never have been. We will never know. He took a vow of silence and celibacy almost 40 years ago and remained in his marriage. They produced two children. One died accidentally at the age of 34. I don't think George and his wife, Clara, ever came to terms with this tragic loss. They simply stopped speaking to each other. George spends his days with his dog and his adult, unmarried, grandson who has emotional and substance abuse problems, but somehow manages to find work in his chosen profession.

George shifted his priorities from son to grandson. He neglected his own son and dedicated himself to doing for his grandson what he could not do for his own son. This includes pampering the boy and denying his bizarre behavior. The grandson is paying a price for this. George thinks he is buying his salvation. He claims to have a "special" relationship with God.

George, a Catholic, says he talks to Jesus and Mary constantly. Clara, in her own room, also talks to Jesus and Mary. She has immersed herself in her religion and is unable to deal with her own tragic reality of her husband. She is in her 70s.

George still remembers how he was verbally abused by his own father and often even beaten with a lash. He never dealt with this pain. He justifies, often quoting the Bible, every aspect of his behavior. He has withdrawn into his own world and is waiting to die.

Aren't there many like George? What a terrible thing religion can be! It is meant to heal us and make us better human beings with the ability to love and forgive each other. He has twisted and perverted his faith. Virtually nothing can get through to him at 80. Is there a cure for people like George who very early in their lives positively influenced the life of so many persons who are now in responsible positions all over the globe? What does Clara do? Her "religion" keeps her from going insane!

ANTHONY AND DEBORAH

Anthony and Deborah, both in their 20s, are brother and sister. Their mother became a single parent after their father died tragically at the age of 30. Anthony was only three when he watched his father die. Deborah was yet to be born. She never knew her father. They have grown up as two delightful young adults who are continuing to grow in their respective careers.

Anthony used to stutter as a child. "My stutter, I believe", he confessed to me, "came as result of the shock and trauma of my father's death. He had just played with me moments before he died."

They apparently had not discussed this part of their lives with a "father figure". Anthony felt that his sister Deborah was rather distant with him. She had a fear of abandonment and was afraid of a long term relationship with a man for fear of abandonment. She felt her Dad had abandoned her.

In her long conversations with me she disclosed that she had tremendous respect for her brother and wanted to get to know him better. They had never gone out together alone for a drink or done something together as brother and sister. She wanted to. Both agreed that they would begin.

BEST FRIENDS FOR OVER SIXTY YEARS

Lucy and Cecilia are both in their 80s. They were classmates at a prestigious girls' Catholic school and had been best friends for over 60 years. Lucy today remains a very docile and sweet woman. Cecilia, on the other hand, is a very angry, resentful, bitter and unforgiving person. She was not so for the first 79 years of her life. She is now 84. She has watched her family completely breakdown as a result of her elder son trying to destroy the younger son out of pure jealousy and rivalry.

She has four children. The other two children have distanced themselves and done little or nothing in Cecilia's eyes. She had poured her heart and soul out to every member of the larger family. No one stood by her and helped her. She and her elder son do not speak to each other. She will not forgive him.

How can a woman like Cecilia heal at age 84? When attempts are made, she growls like a caged animal and cuts off the person trying to get through to her. Her prayers, as a Catholic, are restricted to the only thing she has been taught. She reads her prayers and recites the rosary.

How does Cecilia go to her grave? What can a therapist, priest or anyone tell her?

BRIAN AND DEVIKA

Brian and Devika are South Asians. They are wealthy in their own right and simply stay in their marriage, for convenience. They have been married for over 25 years and have two children. Neither has another lover. They simply have nothing to do with each other. Devika, who is immersed in her career, chooses to live with the pain. She cannot accept what she perceives as the "stigma" of divorce. She is a very proud but good woman. Brian is another story.

ANDREW AND MARIANNE

Andrew and Marianne have been married for over 40 years. They still write notes to each other and occasionally use a friend as a "facilitator"! Marianne is a regular at prayer and healing services. But she refuses to be "healed" as far as the most important person in her life is concerned. Maybe other parts of her life also remain untouched.

BEATRICE

On a flight from Atlanta to Washington DC, I was given a window seat in economy. Business class was full and I had no reservations. An elderly woman sat in the aisle seat in my row. There were three seats and the middle one was empty. Before takeoff, I observed that she was nervous, shaking and staring at me. I asked her what the matter was. She asked me if she could have my seat. I obliged and we exchanged seats.

She explained her trauma to me on the flight. It was incredibly sad. She had three grown up sons and within a period of 90 days, had lost all three of them. Two in a car accident and one was buried alive in a construction site. Two were married and had children. The son who was killed in the construction site was having problems with his wife. They hardly spoke. He had not said goodbye to her for months when he left for work. Strangely, on the day that he died, he had walked up to her, kissed her and told her that he loved her.

The next piece of news that she got during the day, was that her husband was dead. She was in shock.

Beatrice was heavily medicated and now found her only reason to go on living in her Baptist Faith and her grandchildren. I was speechless. How could I say anything when I so very often found myself bickering about things that have gone wrong in my life?

She had wanted my seat because for some reason she felt safer by the window. The tragedies had put a tremendous strain on her marriage of 40 years. She was heading to Washington DC to visit her sister.

For the rest of the flight and for the next three days, I was numb and could only think of Beatrice. I still think of her. What can we learn from this? That tomorrow is guaranteed to no one and may never come. In the words of Kool and the Gang, the legendary music group: "...Cherish the love we have...and cherish every moment we have been given, because time is passing by."

MICHELLE

Michelle is only 17 years old. I knew her parents. For some reason, at a function, she "connected" with me. She pulled me aside and confessed that she was "in love" with a Muslim boy. She was a Catholic and sang in the choir. Her parents were devout Catholics.

Before she went any further, I told her to give up the relationship. I could see what was coming. Her responses to me about her feelings for the young man were at best questionable! She was so young and had so much to look forward to. A relationship and marriage is hard enough for people of the same faith. Often our parents know us best and it is wise to heed their counsel.

In countries that are predominantly non-Christian, the statistics are heavily skewed towards couples of different faiths. I understand this. Some work and some don't. Some are terrific. But when the odds are heavily weighed against you, especially in countries where families and religion play a significant role in marriages, it is best to stand back and consider the coming hardships. In what faith will they raise their children? I know this is very difficult for young people "madly in love" with each other and often extremely painful.

People are or can be beautiful. Marriage is very serious business. It is the most sacred of institutions. It must be considered very seriously.

SANDRA AND A GOD OF SECOND CHANCES

Sandra is 50. She is Chinese American. Having been indulged from a young age she is very spoiled. I got to know her quite a bit while in Chicago and she became a friend. We had no romantic involvement.

Her father left her a lot of money and prime real estate. She has no need to work and has no profession. She was married once which left her bitter. She used to ask me if I could think of one happy marriage! I told her I knew of several happy and healthy marriages where inevitable differences were addressed positively and with love. She disagreed. Her close friends include people of different sexual orientations. Some have no reverence for anything. Life to her and her circle of friends is one funny story. She craves to be the center of attention with one joke after another.

While discussing a certain issue, I told her what she was not used to hearing. Perhaps, my words were not wisely chosen. Perhaps I was a little forceful. I don't think she is used to being corrected. She did not communicate with me after that. I called her, explained what I said, and asked her for forgiveness. I told her I was sorry for what I said to her and asked her to give me a second chance because I valued her friendship. She replied: "I do not give people a second chance!" Our friendship soured.

People like Sandra all over the world, are left bitter by experiences in life and marriage. They remain bitter and rarely become better. What about second chances? Imagine going through life not giving a person a second and many more chances? People find it difficult to give another human being a second chance. Yet, they often worship a "God of second chances" who taught his followers to forgive "not seven times seven, but seventy times seven"!

So many of us like Sandra must take a deep look into our own inner beings and find out why we are the way we are. We think we are free, but we are not. We justify our behavior. Unceasing forgiveness of oneself and others is perhaps the most liberating force. We must accept the reality that to be "truly human and fully alive" we must accept our frailty, that we will fail ourselves and others over and over again in the journey of life. We must embrace the power of forgiveness and second chances in life.

Why do so many people who bury themselves in their places of worship find it hardest to forgive themselves and others, especially those closest to them? This is the heart of every faith.

While addressing a new couple, family and friends at a wedding recently, I reminded the new couple not to be afraid to say "I am sorry; forgive me; I love you" every day. I became a joke to some of the guests. My guess was that these people had never uttered the words "I am sorry" ever in their lives! It is said that these three words are perhaps the most painful to utter between couples and those who care for and love each other.

Is there a Sandra in you? We all deserve more than one chance. In our humanness, no couple can go through life without disappointing one another.

Do we see ourselves in any of these very real stories? We owe it to ourselves not to take any unnecessary baggage to our graves. We have only one life to live on this earth and we must live it fully and abundantly. Marriage partners must focus totally on helping each other become "more than each can be."

|| The Second Or Third Time Around

What can we learn from Sandra? What baggage do we carry from a "bruising" earlier marital relationship? With the divorce rate being at an all-time high in many nations and cultures, how many couples enter into second or third marriages with severe trauma either denied or buried? We know many celebrities and ordinary individuals who are even in their fourth and fifth marriages! Was each prior marriage relationship really irreparable?

Conditional love, as we saw throughout this book, is rather easy. Unconditional love, for the first time, is tough. It can be painful. It requires, above all, letting go of self. Learning to love again can be especially challenging. Avoidance of pain is a national pastime in many cultures. Yet, we are told, that pain and failure can be the greatest teachers. We must not pursue them, but when they do occur, we must embrace them and learn from them.

What role do children play in second and third marriages? The "yours, mine and ours" syndrome is a reality to so many couples. I have seen the terrible chaos and pain this can cause in so many homes. It can also be a source of great blessing but alas this is so very rare.

Children who have gone through the trauma and mixed emotions of the first marriage are so often unable to cope with their new reality. Depending on which parent gets custody of minor children, these little ones end up blaming one of the parents for the failure of the marriage. Sometimes, they blame both. But blame does not solve the problem.

When a new Dad or Mum enters their lives, the affected children often respond with anger and cynicism. If the new step-parent brings his or her children, the situation in the new home can be tense. There are however situations where everybody in the new home lives "happily ever after". But this is so rare.

Whenever a couple is faced with a "yours and mine" situation, they must let the children get to know each other if the children would be living under the same roof. This must happen even if the children live in different homes. They are part of the same family now. A family that is also "new". The new partners must also see the scars, if any, in each other's children, and decide with their heads and hearts if they still want a life together.

In many cultures, as we saw earlier, the extended family is an integral part of society. When two people enter into a marriage relationship, they also "marry" the extended family, especially each other's parents and siblings. This is also increasingly a vital part of the social fabric in both the evolving American and Western societies. In nations where there is no effective system to take care of the elderly, it is the children's duty to provide this. Yes, even after marriage. This can be a real challenge to couples in many cultures including America and the West. What is an American today? An Englishman? A German? Inter-cultural marriages are so common.

Letting go of the past has been the subject of many books and research by very smart individuals. Yet, this still remains the hardest thing to do for so many of us. Letting go of the past must begin not with denial but with a totally acceptance of this past with all it's "horrors" and failures.

In the first chapter of this book, "It takes to Tango", I cited the lesson to be learned from the world of international relations, with the final meeting between the then UN Secretary General and the late Iraqi President before the war began. In addition to counseling, by accident or design, so many individuals and couples in different cultures, I have been a student and practitioner of international relations and international business for the last 25 years. Letting go of the past was perhaps the biggest challenge faced even by world leaders. British Prime Minister Tony Blair, who captured with his charisma the imagination of most British and world citizens in his first years in office, had this to say when he was faced with the reality of being swept out of office: 'Letting go is hard. But sometimes, it is the right thing to do". True, he saw the writing on the wall. Today, he is more effective than ever before and doing more good globally especially in the Middle East and Africa.

Yet another outstanding example of this is former US President Bill Clinton. Only he could have pulled off such a resurrection! He had what it takes. I also think that the "stars" were aligned in his favor! He also had to let go of a "past" that captured the world's attention for years. Today, he is perhaps the most sought after and effective speaker in the world in addition to leading a global organization, the Clinton Global Initiative, which is doing so much good in the world.

Former US President Jimmy Carter is another example who was seen as a "failed" President but became a terrific former President.

There are however some world and business leaders who simply refuse to face their reality and let go. They cling to office, crippling nations and organizations. Letting go also takes extraordinary courage.

I realize I have given examples of "letting go" from world celebrities. Yet, I have met and worked with so many ordinary individuals who have done extraordinary things by simply letting go of the past.

Let us learn from Bette Midler again in her song, "The Rose". "Some say love, it is a razor that leaves your soul to bleed......it's the heart afraid of breaking, that never learns to dance......it's a dream afraid of waking, that never takes a chance......and the soul afraid of dying, that never learns to live".

Fear. Fear of loving again unconditionally. What a crippling and destructive emotion! We must face this fear in our relationships, embrace and let go of the past, and learn to love unconditionally and live fully again.

PERSONAL REFLECTION AND DISCUSSION
BETWEEN PARTNERS

Q: If I am entering into a second or third marriage, have I faced the reality of my mistakes in the earlier relationship?

A: _____

_____

Q: What are the mistakes I made? Will I make the same mistakes again?

A: _____

_____

Q: What was right and what was wrong in this earlier marriage or relationship?

A: _____

_____

Q: Have I accepted my share of responsibility for the failure of the earlier marriage?

A: _____

_____

Q: Am I shifting any blame to my earlier partner or spouse?

A: _____

_____

Q: What have I learned from the earlier marriage or relationship?

A: _____

_____

Q: Have I rid myself of all the negative and crippling baggage and emotions from my previous relationship before entering into my new relationship?

A: _____

_____

Q: If minor children are involved in a "yours, mine and even ours" relationship, have I embraced this new reality with all the good, the bad and the ugly?

A: _____

_____

Q: Am I really ready to love unconditionally again?

A: _____

‖ Concluding Thoughts

At the beginning of this book, I emphasized that my goal was to keep the book simple. I do hope that it has touched the lives of some couples and made their relationships better. The feedback from the Asian edition was very positive, despite the cynics who are everywhere! The questions at the end of each chapter for partners have had a powerful impact on many. So often when we see ourselves in the characters in a book and it is not to our liking, we attack the author instead of learning from it. We all must accept our flaws, learn from them and become better human beings especially as life partners and as parents.

So much has been written on this subject, yet the divorce rates in the US and globally seem to be rising. Why?

I have spent much of my life in the US and in several Asian countries. I am also acquainted with the Latin American cultures. The ten rules that I have cited apply to every culture. Questions one and two in rule four apply to every human being anywhere.

I have spent time working in refugee camps where people were left with nothing except each other and little or no hope. Let me repeat the questions for emphasis: 1. Do I believe that every minute, every moment of my life is a gift? 2. Do I believe that my partner's life or my life could end any moment? I would add a third question: "how will my behavior change today if I knew that my partner had one week to live"? These three questions alone if answered honestly together by both partners anywhere in the world will make a difference in any marriage or relationship.

There will always be some who will scoff at these questions and walk away from them. There are always some who are simply out of reach. It takes two to tango; to dance together. Both partners but must be willing participants and committed to the relationship which cannot and must not be conditional.

The moment one human being expects something from another human being forever, the stage is set for disappointment and trouble. No two human beings can always fully satisfy one another and meet each other's expectations in this 24/7 world! The only people who profit from the inevitable disharmony and conflict are the mental health professionals!

I hope that this little book, however flawed, has had a positive impact on every person who reads it and that something has been learned to make the reader a better partner, parent and human being.

I may have oversimplified a very complex subject. My intent is to keep the book simple and readable, and also to provoke discussion between intended and married partners, and society as a whole. If one marriage or relationship is improved, saved or restored in some corner of the world because of this book, then my work would not have been in vain.

How do you improve or save innumerable marriages and relationships in crisis, trouble or those that simply need improvement? One at a time.

Good luck!

wide, is a keynote speaker at several global forums and has been published and interviewed in the global media. He was Public Relations Chairman, Los Angeles Chapter of the National Speakers Association. He lives in Southern California and Colombo, Sri Lanka, where he directs the South Asia operations of his organization and has completed research for an upcoming management book. He can be reached via e mail: gerardmuttukumaru@yahoo.com.

About the Author

Gerard D. Muttukumaru holds a Master of Commerce degree with specialization in Business and Organization Psychology from Loyola College, University of Madras, India and a Master of Business Administration degree with a specialization in Marketing and International Business from the Merrick School of Business, University of Baltimore, Maryland, US. He is the Founder and Chairman of the USA based Center for Global Leadership Worldwide, a global customized executive education, management consulting and corporate training organization with representative offices worldwide.

In the US, he has taught Cross-Cultural Management, Leadership, Change, Strategy, Organization Behavior, Performance Management and Global Business in undergraduate, MBA and Executive Education Programs for over 15 years. He has served on the adjunct faculty of the University of California, Riverside and the University of Phoenix in Southern California. His students included senior and mid-level managers from major organizations in the USA such as Disney, Bank of America, Wells Fargo Bank, Warner, Northrop, Lockheed, ARCO and Silicon Valley companies. In addition, he has lived and worked in numerous countries and counseled managers from almost every continent in career guidance, conflict management, collaboration, interpersonal communication, leadership and behavior change. He has also worked with numerous couples throughout the world on marriage and family issues.

While serving on the Boards of several community and civic organizations in Southern California, he has counseled numerous young individuals and couples on life and career issues. He is the author of "Rethinking your Life in the New New World – how the new global economy affects everyone" published in 2005 by the Malaysian Institute of Management. A US and western edition is in progress. He continues to address management audiences world-